Mike McGrath & Michael Price

Microsoft Excel

In easy steps is an imprint of In Easy Steps Limited
16 Hamilton Terrace · Holly Walk · Leamington Spa
Warwickshire · United Kingdom · CV32 4LY
www.ineasysteps.com

Notice of Liability
Every effort has been made to ensure that this book contains accurate
and current information. However, In Easy Steps Limited and the
author shall not be liable for any loss or damage suffered by readers
as a result of any information contained herein.

Trademarks
Microsoft® and Windows® are registered trademarks of Microsoft
Corporation. All other trademarks are acknowledged as belonging to
their respective companies.

In Easy Steps Limited supports The Forest Stewardship Council (FSC),
the leading international forest certification organization. All our titles
that are printed on Greenpeace approved FSC certified paper carry the
FSC logo.

MIX
Paper from
responsible sources
FSC® C020837

Printed and bound in the United Kingdom

ISBN 978-1-84078-996-6

Contents

7   Control Excel   105

8   Charts   123

1 Introduction

This chapter shows how the spreadsheet – the electronic counterpart of the paper ledger – has evolved in Excel, taking advantage of the various features of Microsoft Office and the Windows operating system.

The Spreadsheet Concept

Spreadsheets, in the guise of the accountant's ledger sheet, have been in use for many, many years. They originally consisted of paper forms with a two-dimensional grid of rows and columns, often on extra-large paper, forming two pages of a ledger book, for example (hence the term "spread sheet"). They were typically used by accountants to prepare budget or financial statements. Each row would represent a different item, with each column showing the value or amount for that item over a given time period. For example, a forecast for a 30% margin (mark-up) and 10% growth might look like this:

Margin %	30					
Growth %	10					
				Profit Forecast		
		January	February	March	April	May
Cost of Goods		6,000	6,600	7,260	7,986	8,785
Sales		7,800	8,580	9,438	10,382	11,420
Profit		1,800	1,980	2,178	2,396	2,635
Total Profit		1,800	3,780	5,958	8,354	10,989

Any changes to the basic figures would mean that all the values would have to be recalculated and transcribed to another ledger sheet to show the effect – e.g. for a 20% margin and 60% growth:

Margin %	20					
Growth %	60					
				Profit Forecast		
		January	February	March	April	May
Cost of Goods		6,000	9,600	15,360	24,576	39,322
Sales		7,200	11,520	18,432	29,491	47,186
Profit		1,200	1,920	3,072	4,915	7,864
Total Profit		1,200	3,120	6,192	11,107	18,972

To make another change (for example, to show a 10% margin and 200% growth) would involve a completely new set of calculations and each time there would be the possibility of a calculation or transcription error creeping in.

With the advent of the personal computer a new approach became possible. Applications were developed to simulate the operation of the financial ledger sheet, but the boxes (known as cells) that formed the rows and columns could store text, numbers, or a calculation formula based on the contents of other cells. The spreadsheet looked the same, since it was the results that were displayed rather than the formulas themselves. However, when the contents of a cell were changed in the spreadsheet, all cells whose values depended on that changed cell would be automatically recalculated.

Hot tip

Ledger sheets pre-date computers and handheld calculators, and have been in use for literally hundreds of years.

Hot tip

The first spreadsheet application was VisiCorp's VisiCalc (visible calculator). Numerous competitive programs appeared, but market leadership was taken first by Lotus 1-2-3, and now by Microsoft Excel.

...cont'd

This new approach allowed a vast improvement in productivity for various activities, such as forecasting. In the second example shown on the previous page, you'd set up the initial spreadsheet using formulas, rather than calculating the individual cell values. A spreadsheet might contain these values and formulas like this:

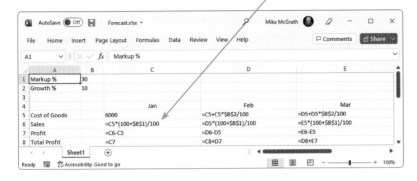

Don't forget

The = sign signals to Excel that what follows is a formula and must be calculated.

However, what will be displayed in the cells are the actual values that the formulas compute, based on the contents of the cells that the formulas refer to:

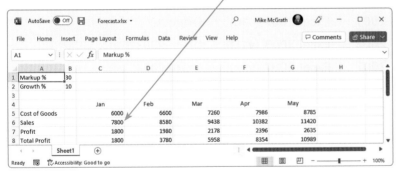

Hot tip

Sets of predefined functions were added, plus support for writing small programs, or macros, to manipulate the data. Further developments incorporated graphs, images, and audio.

When you want to see the effect of changes (for example, to show different values for margin and growth), you change just those items and instantly see the effect as the values calculated by the formulas are adjusted and redisplayed. The capabilities of the spreadsheet applications have evolved, and the use of spreadsheets has extended far beyond the original use for financial planning and reporting. They can now handle any activity that involves arrays of values interrelated by formulas, such as grading examination scores, interpreting experimental data, or keeping track of assets and inventories. In fact, the newest spreadsheet applications seem to support just about any possible requirement that can be imagined.

Microsoft Excel

Microsoft Excel

VisiCalc and Lotus 1-2-3 were MS-DOS programs, subject to its command-line interface, but Microsoft Excel was developed for Windows. It was the first spreadsheet program to allow users to control the visual aspects of the spreadsheet (fonts, character attributes, cell appearance, etc.). It introduced intelligent cell recomputation, where only cells dependent on the cell being modified are updated (previous spreadsheet programs recomputed everything all the time, or waited for a specific Recalc command). Versions of Excel for Microsoft Windows and Office include:

Year	Version	Name
1987	Excel 2.0	[Windows]
1990	Excel 3.0	[Windows]
1992	Excel 4.0	[Windows]
1993	Excel 5.0	[Windows]
1995	Excel 95 (v7.0)	Office 95
1997	Excel 97 (v8.0)	Office 97
1999	Excel 2000 (v9.0)	Office 2000
2001	Excel 2002 (v10)	Office XP
2003	Excel 2003 (v11)	Office 2003
2007	Excel 2007 (v12)	Office 2007
2010	Excel 2010 (v14)	Office 2010
2013	Excel 2013 (v15)	Office 2013 / Office 365
2015	Excel 2016 (v16)	Office 2016 / Office 365
2018	Excel 2019 (v16)	Office 2019 / Office 365
2021	Excel 2021 (v16)	Office 2021/365
2022	Excel 2021 (v16)	Microsoft 365 Office

Hot tip

There are also versions of Excel designed specifically for Apple Macintosh ("Mac") computers – starting from Excel 1.0! Excel is also available in versions for mobile devices that use iOS, such as the iPad and the iPhone. Plus, there are versions for cell phones and tablets that are Android- or Windows-based.

The newer versions of Excel provide many enhancements to the user interface, and incorporate connections with other Microsoft Office/365 applications. The basis of the program, however, remains the same. It still consists of a large array of cells, organized into rows and columns, containing data values or formulas with relative or absolute references to other cells. This means that many of the techniques included in this book are applicable to whichever version of Excel you may be using, or even if you are using a spreadsheet from another product – although the specifics of the instructions may need to be adjusted.

Microsoft 365

Later versions of Excel were shipped as part of the bundled stand-alone Microsoft Office suite of applications, which included programs like Microsoft Word and Microsoft PowerPoint.

Subsequently, Microsoft released a subscription version of the Office suite of applications, named Office 365. This was available as an alternative to the stand-alone version. One great advantage of Office 365 was that apps got updated automatically via Windows Update to ensure you always had the latest features. After the release of Office 365, the Excel version remains 16.0.

Microsoft Office

Microsoft Office 2021 was the final version of the stand-alone Microsoft Office suite of applications. Its components are thereafter available in the Microsoft 365 subscription version, which replaces the Office 365 subscription version.

Microsoft 365 is available in these individual user editions:
- **Microsoft 365 Personal** (formerly Office 365 Personal)
- **Microsoft 365 Family** (formerly Office 365 Home)

There are also several editions for larger organizations, including:
- **Microsoft 365 Business Standard**
- **Microsoft 365 Enterprise Apps**
- **Microsoft 365 Education**

Microsoft 365

All these editions include the fully-featured Microsoft Excel app, which uses a result-oriented interface with Ribbon, File tab, Backstage, Galleries, and Live Preview.

Excel uses the OpenXML file format by default. This is based on XML and uses ZIP compression to create files up to 75% smaller than those in the older Microsoft Office file formats. Shared features include Document Theme, which defines colors, fonts, and graphic effects, and collaboration services for sharing spreadsheets and documents with other users.

Excel Online
Microsoft offers free web-based versions of Excel, Word, and more. These online apps have interfaces similar to the desktop products, and allow access to Excel spreadsheets and documents via your browser. They make it easy to share documents with users who may not have a Microsoft 365 subscription, but the online apps may not support the full feature-set of the desktop products.

The Microsoft 365 Online apps work in conjunction with OneDrive, the online storage associated with your Microsoft account.

System Requirements

To install and run Microsoft 365 with Excel, your computer should match or better these minimum hardware and operating system requirements:

Computer and processor
- Windows OS: 1.6GHz, 2-core.
- macOS: Intel processor.

Memory
- Windows OS: 4GB RAM; 2GB RAM (32-bit).
- macOS: 4GB RAM.

Hard disk
- Windows OS: 4GB of available space.
- macOS: 10GB available space, Extended Format (HFS+).

Monitor
- Windows OS: 1278 x 768 screen resolution.
- macOS: 1280 x 800 screen resolution.

Don't forget

The 64-bit version of Microsoft 365 will be automatically installed unless you explicitly select the 32-bit version.

Hot tip

A broadband internet connection is recommended for download, product activation, and for OneDrive online storage.

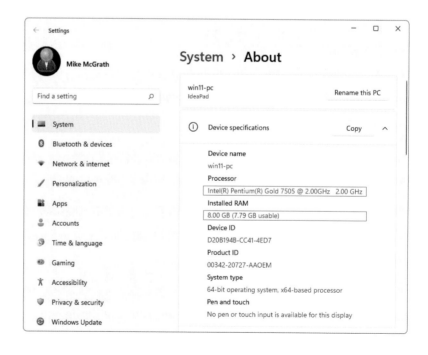

Getting Excel

Excel is a part of the Microsoft 365 suite of Office applications. Microsoft 365 is available only as a subscription model that provides regular updates as new features are introduced. There are several versions of Microsoft 365 for Home and Business users. You can decide which version is best for you by visiting the comparison website at **microsoft.com/en-ww/microsoft-365/ buy/compare-all-microsoft-365-products**

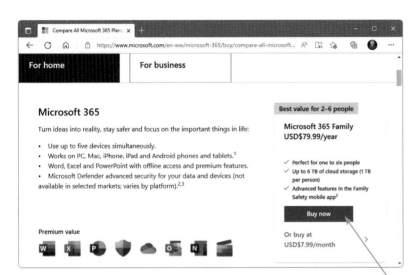

Hot tip

You may also find a tile on your Start menu that you can click to get started with a Microsoft 365 subscription.

Microsoft 365 (Office)

At the time of writing, the popular available versions of Microsoft 365 subscriptions are those listed in the table below:

Hot tip

Click the **Buy now** button beside your preferred version to begin completion of the Microsoft 365 subscription process.

Version	Features
Microsoft 365 Personal	For 1 person, 1TB of cloud storage
Microsoft 365 Family	For 1-6 people, 1TB of cloud storage per person
Microsoft 365 Business Basic	Each user, web & mobile Office apps only, 1TB of cloud storage per user
Microsoft 365 Apps for business	Each user, desktop Office apps, 1TB of cloud storage per user
Microsoft 365 Business Standard	For 5 mobile, tablet, and PC devices, 1TB of cloud storage per user
Microsoft 365 Business Premium	For 5 mobile, tablet, and PC devices, 1TB of cloud storage per user, Advanced security

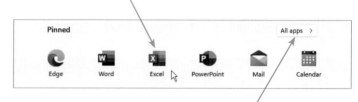

Excel and Windows

With Microsoft 365 installed under Windows, you have a number of ways to launch Excel:

1 You may find tiles for the Office applications on the **Start** screen. Click the Excel tile

2 If a tile isn't shown, select the **All apps** list then scroll to the **E** category and click the **Excel** entry

You can also look for applications by name, using Windows' **Search** feature:

1 Click the **Search** button on the Windows desktop taskbar

2 Type "excel" in the **Search** box to find matching items

3 Select the **Excel** app entry in the search results to launch the application

If you have a microphone on your system, you can use **Cortana** to simply ask to start applications:

1 Go to **Settings**, **Privacy & security**, **Voice activation** and ensure that **Cortana** is set to respond to voice commands

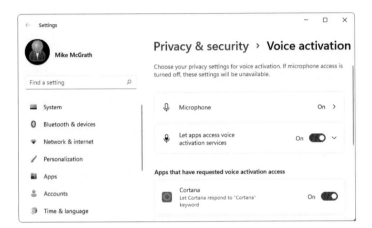

If Cortana can't hear you, go to **Settings**, **Privacy & security**, **Microphone** and turn **On** the **Let apps access your microphone**, **Cortana** option.

2 Select **Cortana** on the **All apps** list, or say "Hey Cortana" into your system microphone, to wake up **Cortana**

3 Now, say "start Excel" into the microphone to launch the Excel app

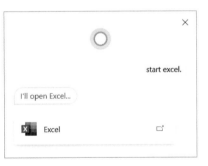

Whichever technique you use, the Excel app will be loaded and made ready to deal with your requirements.

Cortana's performance may vary by region. If Cortana is not working or enabled in your country, try setting your region to "United States" in **Settings**, **Time & language**, **Language & region**.

The Excel Ribbon

The menus and toolbars used in earlier versions of Excel have been replaced by the Ribbon. With this, commands are organized into logical groups, under command tabs named **Home**, **Insert**, **Page Layout**, **Formulas**, **Data**, **Review**, **View** and **Help** – arranged in the order in which tasks are often performed. When you click any of these tabs, the corresponding commands display in the Ribbon.

The Ribbon may also include contextual command tabs, which appear when you perform a specific task. For example, if you select some data and then click **Insert Column or Bar Chart**, **2D-Column** in the **Charts** group, chart tool tabs **Format** and **Chart Design** are displayed.

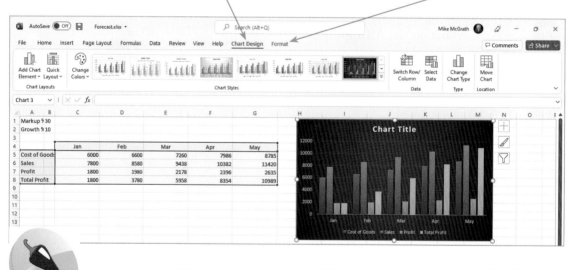

Hot tip

You can also choose **Full-screen mode** to run Excel full-screen, with no tabs or commands visible. Click the top of the app to display the Ribbon.

You can minimize the Ribbon, to use more of the space on the screen for the actual content of the spreadsheet:

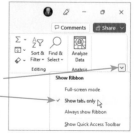

1 Click the **Ribbon Display Options** button and select **Show tabs only** – the tabs will still be displayed but the commands will be hidden

Other Microsoft 365 apps such as Word, Access and PowerPoint also have a Ribbon – displaying tabs appropriate to those particular apps.

2 The Ribbon and the commands are redisplayed as a temporary overlay whenever you click a tab, or when you use the **Alt** key shortcuts (see page 118)

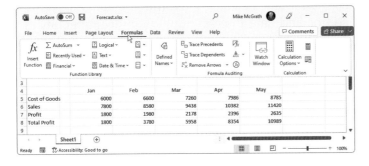

Touch/Mouse Mode

Excel offers two interfaces – Mouse or Touch, where the latter is optimized for touch-enabled devices. To enable Touch Mode:

1 Click the **Ribbon Display Options** button and select **Show Quick Access Toolbar** – a toolbar containing a drop-down arrow button now appears below the Ribbon

The **File** tab displays the Backstage view, which provides general document file functions and options. For example, **Options**, **Quick Access Toolbar** can be used to add items you regularly use to the Quick Access Toolbar so that they are readily available.

2 Click the drop-down arrow button on the Quick Access Toolbar, then choose the **Touch/Mouse Mode** option to add that item to the Quick Access Toolbar

3 Click the **Touch/Mouse Mode** item on the Quick Access Toolbar – see the Ribbon now display with extra spacing

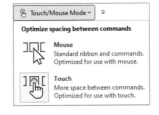

17

Exploring Excel

If you are used to a previous version of Excel you may not always know where to find the features you need. The following table lists some of the actions that you may want to carry out, and indicates the Ribbon tabs and groups where the associated commands for these actions may be found in Excel:

Action	Tab	Groups
Create, open, save, print, share, or export files – or change options	**File**	Backstage Commands: New, Open, Info, Save, Save As, Print, Share, Export, Publish, Close, Account, Options, and Feedback
Format, insert, delete, edit or find data in cells, columns, and rows	**Home**	Font, Alignment, Number, Styles, Cells, Editing, Analysis
Create tables, charts, sparklines, reports, slicers, and hyperlinks	**Insert**	Tables, Add-ins, Charts, Tours, Sparklines, Filters, Links
Set page margins, page breaks, print areas, or sheet options	**Page Layout**	Themes, Page Setup, Scale to Fit, Sheet Options, Arrange
Find functions, define names, or troubleshoot formulas	**Formulas**	Function Library, Defined Names, and Formula Auditing, Calculation
Import or connect to data, sort and filter data, validate data, flash fill values, or perform a What-If Analysis	**Data**	Get & Transform Data, Queries & Connections, Data Types, Sort & Filter, Data Tools, Forecast
Check spelling, review and revise, and protect a sheet or workbook	**Review**	Proofing, Comments, Notes, Protect
Change workbook views, arrange windows, freeze panes, and record macros	**View**	Sheet View, Workbook Views, Show, Zoom, Window, Macros

Hot tip

Explore the Ribbon tabs and command groups in Excel to find the features that you need to carry out activities on your worksheets.

Hot tip

There is a **Search** box above the Excel Ribbon where you can enter words and phrases, to quickly locate features or get help on what you want to do.

If you want to locate a particular command, you can search a list of all the commands that are available in Excel:

1 Click the drop-down arrow button on the Quick Access Toolbar, then choose the **More Commands** option to open the "Customize the Quick Access Toolbar" menu

2 Click the drop-down arrow button in the **Choose commands from** box, then select **All Commands**

You can alternatively click **File**, **Options**, **Quick Access Toolbar** to open the "Customize the Quick Access Toolbar" menu.

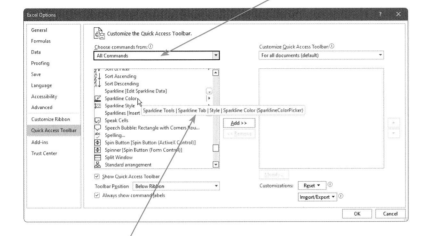

To list commands that may not be currently in any group, you can select **Commands Not in the Ribbon**.

3 A **ScreenTip** will indicate the tab and group containing that command as you scroll down the list and move the mouse pointer over a command name

4 Some commands may not currently be included in any group, and so will be shown with just their name – for example, the **Calculator** command

You can also right-click the Ribbon and select **Customize the Ribbon...** to display a list of commands and view the associated ScreenTips.

5 Click **Add**, **OK** to add a selected command to the Quick Access Toolbar – for example, **AutoFit Column Width**

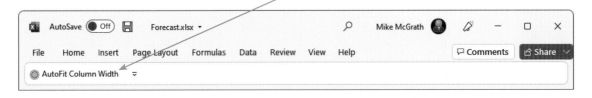

Excel Online App

1 To use the free Microsoft 365 Online apps, open your web browser and visit **microsoft. com/en-us/microsoft-365/ free-office-online-for-the- web**, then sign in with your Microsoft account

2 Select **Excel** from the choice of Microsoft 365 Online apps

Microsoft 365 Online apps are touch-friendly web applications that let you create, edit and share Excel, Word, PowerPoint and OneNote files from any browser. They are free to use and can share your OneDrive storage. However, the web page and the steps for accessing the free apps may vary.

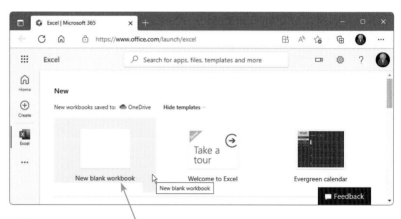

3 Select the **New blank workbook** option – to begin working on a new spreadsheet

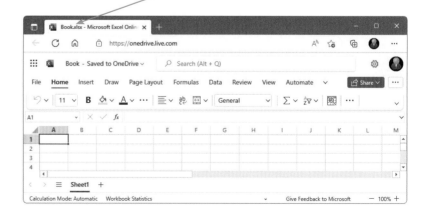

2 Begin with Excel

We start with a simple workbook, to show what's involved in entering, modifying, and formatting data, and in performing calculations. This includes ways in which Excel helps to minimize the effort. We cover printing, look at Excel Help, and discuss the various file formats associated with Excel.

The Excel Window

When you launch Excel, you usually start with the Excel window displaying a blank workbook called "Book1":

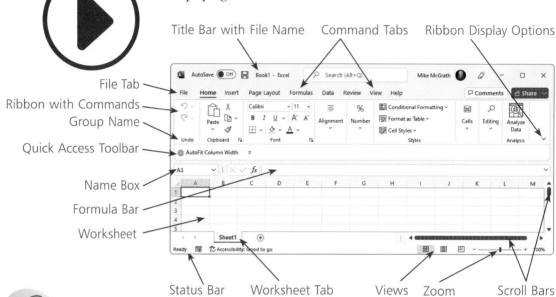

Title Bar with File Name   Command Tabs   Ribbon Display Options

File Tab
Ribbon with Commands
Group Name
Quick Access Toolbar
Name Box
Formula Bar
Worksheet

Status Bar   Worksheet Tab   Views   Zoom   Scroll Bars

Don't forget

Each workbook opens in its own window, making it easier to switch between workbooks when you have several open at the same time.

Hot tip

The **Home** tab contains all the commands for basic worksheet activities, in the **Clipboard**, **Font**, **Alignment**, **Number**, **Styles**, **Cells**, and **Editing** groups.

1 Move the mouse over a command icon in one of the groups to see the command description – for example, **Home** (tab), [**Alignment**] (group), **Top Align** (command)

2 Click the drop-down arrow next to a command (e.g. **Merge & Center**) to show related commands

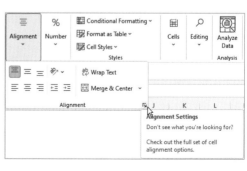

3 Click the arrow button in the bottom corner of the group options to see a dialog box providing even more options

...cont'd

By default, Excel provides one array of data (called a worksheet) in the workbook. This is named "Sheet1". Click the **+** button beside the worksheet tab to add more worksheets.

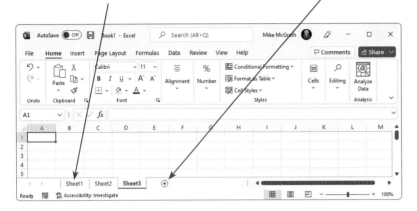

One worksheet is usually all you need to create a spreadsheet, but it can sometimes be convenient to organize the data into several worksheets.

Each worksheet is the equivalent of a full spreadsheet and has the potential for up to 1,048,576 x 16,384 cells, arranged in rows and columns. The rows are numbered **1, 2, 3** and onward, up to a maximum of 1,048,576. The columns are lettered **A** to **Z, AA** to **ZZ**, and then **AAA** to **XFD**. This gives a maximum of 16,384 columns. The combination gives a unique reference for each cell, from **A1** right up to **XFD1048576**. Only very few of these cells will be visible at any one time, but any part of the worksheet can be displayed on the screen, which acts as a rectangular "porthole" onto the whole worksheet. The actual number of cells shown depends on screen resolution, cell size, and display mode (e.g. with Ribbon minimized or full-screen).

These are the theoretical limits for worksheets. For very large numbers of records, a database program may be a more suitable choice.

23

Use the scroll bars to reposition the screen view, or type a cell reference into the Name box. For example, type **ZN255**.

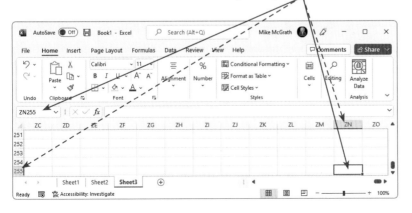

See pages 44-45 for other ways to navigate through the worksheet using arrow keys, scroll functions, split views, keystrokes, the mouse, and touch.

Create a Workbook

You can begin by creating a simple, personal budget workbook, to illustrate the processes involved in creating and updating an Excel spreadsheet.

1 When Excel opens, it offers a list of recent workbooks and allows you to open other workbooks. For a new workbook you could choose a template appropriate to your purpose. As your starting point, simply select **Blank workbook**, which will be named "Book1" by default

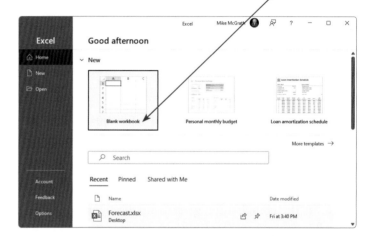

2 Type the spreadsheet title "My Personal Budget" in cell **A1** and press the **Down** arrow, or the **Enter** key, to go to cell **A2** (or just click cell **A2** to select it)

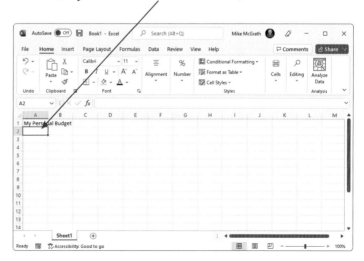

Hot tip

The Excel Start screen displays templates, and lists recent workbooks. You could select a predefined workbook template from those stored on your computer or online at the Microsoft website.

Don't forget

Text is automatically aligned to the left of the cell; numbers are aligned to the right.

Add Data to the Worksheet

1 Continue to add text to the cells in column **A**, pressing the **Down** arrow key or **Enter** to move down after each, to create labels in cells **A2** to **A13**:

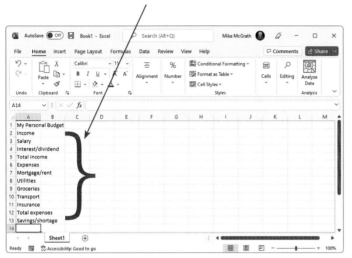

Income
Salary
Interest/dividend
Total income
Expenses
Mortgage/rent
Utilities
Groceries
Transport
Insurance
Total expenses
Savings/shortage

2 Click the **File** tab, and select **Save** (or press the **Ctrl + S** keyboard shortcut)

3 Select a location (in OneDrive or on your computer), then type a file name – e.g. "My Personal Budget"

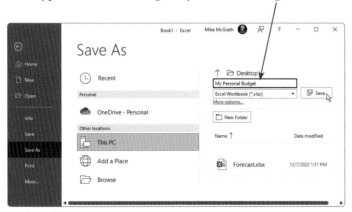

4 Click the **Save** button to add the workbook to the selected location with your given file name

Hot tip

If text is available in another document, you can copy and paste the text, to save typing.

Beware

The first time you save a workbook, **Save As** gets called so that you can name the workbook. You should save the workbook regularly while creating or updating spreadsheets, to avoid losing your work if a system problem arises.

Build the Worksheet

You can fill in the columns of data for each month of the year, but first you need to add an extra row after the title for the column headings. To add a row to the worksheet:

1 Select the row (click the row number) above where you want to insert another row – for example, select row **2**

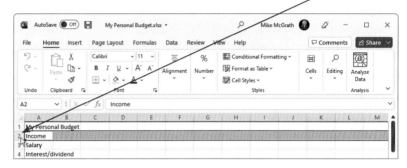

Hot tip

To insert multiple rows, select a block of as many rows as you need, and then click **Insert** – the new rows will be inserted above the selection. Use a similar procedure to insert one or more new columns.

2 Click the **Home** tab, then in the [**Cells**] group, click the arrow beside **Insert**, and click **Insert Sheet Rows**

3 Click cell **B2** in the new row, and type "January", then press **Enter** twice to move to **B4**

4 Type 3950 in cell **B4**, press **Enter**, type 775 in cell **B5**, and press **Enter** again

5 In cell **B6** type **=** then click in **B4** and type **+**. Click **B5** (to get **=B4+B5**) then press **Enter** to see the total appear in **B6**

Don't forget

The **=** symbol signifies that what follows is a formula. This creates a formula in cell **B6**, to specify that Total income = Salary plus Interest/dividend. Excel automatically calculates the result and displays it in cell **B6**. Select the cell and look in the Formula bar to see the formula.

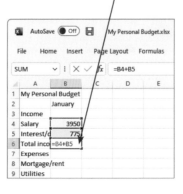

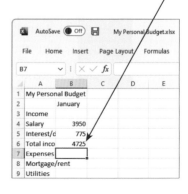

6 Click cell **B8**, and then type the values 2250, 425, 1150, 350, and 450 (pressing the **Down** arrow key or **Enter** after each)

7 In cell **B13**, type **=SUM(** and then click **B8**, type a **:** colon character, click **B12**, type **)** and press **Enter**, then click **B13** to see the **Formula bar** contents

You can click **B13**, then click the **Σ AutoSum** button in the [**Editing**] group on the **Home** tab. This automatically sums the adjacent cells – in this case, the five cells above, giving **=SUM(B8:B12)**. See page 68 for more details on **AutoSum**.

Some of the labels in column **A** appear truncated. The full label is still recorded, but the part that overlapped column **B** cannot be displayed if the adjacent cell is occupied.

To change the column width to fit the contents:

1 Select the column of labels (click the letter heading)

2 On the **Home** tab, in the [**Cells**] group, select **Format**

3 Under **Cell Size**, select **AutoFit Column Width**

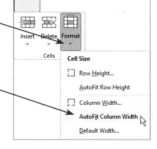

4 Alternatively, move the mouse pointer over the column boundary, and drag to manually widen – or double-click to **AutoFit** to the cell contents

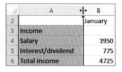

Column width is measured in characters (assuming a standard font). The default is 8.43, but you can set any value from 0 to 255.

To change a group of columns, select the first, hold down **Shift** and select the last. For non-adjacent columns, select the first, hold down **Ctrl** and click other columns.

27

Fill Cells

You typed "January", but the rest of the monthly headings can be automatically completed, using the **Fill Handle** to enter data, following the pattern it recognizes in your existing cell data:

1 Select the **B2** cell with the "January" heading

2 Move the mouse to the bottom-right corner of the cell to see the + **Fill Handle** appear

3 Click the **Fill Handle** and drag over adjacent cells to select them, then release the mouse button to fill those cells

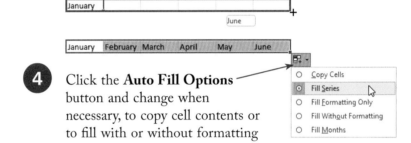

4 Click the **Auto Fill Options** button and change when necessary, to copy cell contents or to fill with or without formatting

Excel recognizes various entry types. If you start with "Jan" rather than "January", adjacent cells fill with "Feb", "Mar", "Apr", etc.

5 Select cell **B4**, and fill cells **C4:G4** with a copy of **B4**. Repeat for **B6** to **C6:G6**, and for **B13** to **C13:G13**. Select the block of cells **B8:B9**, and fill cells **C8:G9**

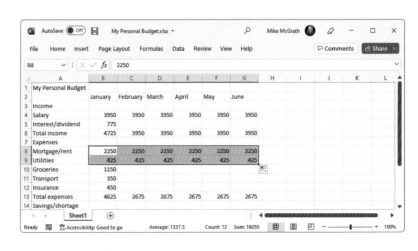

Hot tip

You can also use the right-click menu to edit (cut/copy/delete) a selection of cells and to insert copied cells at another location. Just select the cell(s) with the mouse and right-click to see the options available.

Don't forget

Formulas are adjusted to show the column change; e.g. **=B4+B5** will become **=C4+C5**, **=D4+D5**, etc. See page 61 for more details on this effect, which is called relative referencing.

Complete the Worksheet

1 Select cell **H2**, and type "Period" as the heading

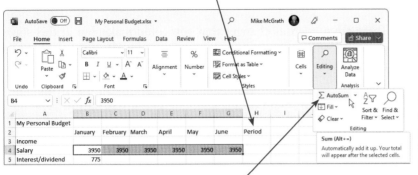

Don't forget

It is sometimes more efficient to fill a whole range of cells, then clear the ones that are not necessary.

2 Select cells **B4** to **G4**, click **AutoSum** in [**Editing**], on the **Home** tab, and see that the total gets entered in cell **H4**

3 Select cell **H4** and autofill **H5** to **H14**, then select **H7** and press **Delete** (no values to total)

	H
2	Period
3	
4	23700
5	775
6	24475
7	
8	13500
9	2550
10	1150
11	350
12	450
13	18000
14	0
15	18000

4 Select cell **B14**, type **=B6-B13**, then press **Enter** (type the whole formula, or select the cells to add their addresses)

5 Select cell **B14**, then drag and fill to copy the formula for Total income minus Total expenses to the cells **C13:G14**

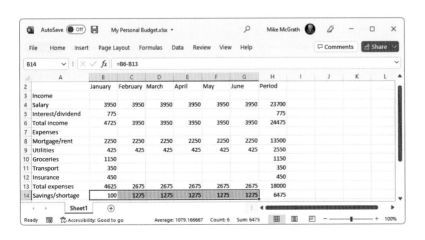

Hot tip

You can right-click the tab for Sheet1 and select **Rename**, calling it "My Personal Budget", for example.

29

Format the Text

Although not essential for the functionality of the spreadsheet, formatting the text can make it easier to view the workbook, and make prints more readable.

There are numerous changes that you could make, but at this stage you can just make some changes to font size and styles, and to the text placement:

Hot tip

The worksheet changes momentarily as you move over the font sizes, showing you how the change would affect the appearance.

Beware

You may need to reapply **AutoFit** when you make changes to the font size and style for labels or to the format for data columns.

1 Click cell **A3**, press and hold **Ctrl**, and click cells **A6**, **A7**, **A13** and **A14**. Click the **Home** tab, [**Font**] group, **Font Settings** arrow, then select size 14 and click the **Bold** font button

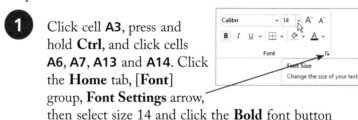

2 Click column label cell **B2**, press **Shift** and click cell **H2**, then select font size 14, **Bold** for cells **B2:H2**, and select **Home,** [**Alignment**], **Align Right**

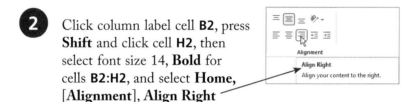

3 Select cell range **A1** to **H1**, then select **Home,** [**Alignment**], **Merge & Center** and choose font size 20, and **Bold** for the workbook title

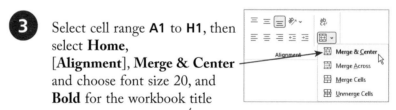

Don't forget

Whenever you make changes, click the **Save** button on the Excel Title bar to store the workbook so that updates won't be lost.

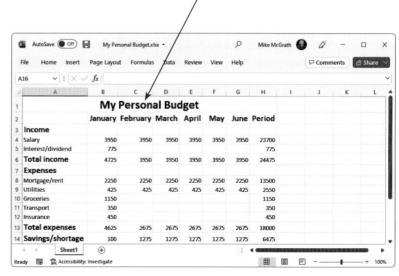

	A	B	C	D	E	F	G	H
1		My Personal Budget						
2		January	February	March	April	May	June	Period
3	**Income**							
4	Salary	3950	3950	3950	3950	3950	3950	23700
5	Interest/dividend	775						775
6	**Total income**	4725	3950	3950	3950	3950	3950	24475
7	**Expenses**							
8	Mortgage/rent	2250	2250	2250	2250	2250	2250	13500
9	Utilities	425	425	425	425	425	425	2550
10	Groceries	1150						1150
11	Transport	350						350
12	Insurance	450						450
13	**Total expenses**	4625	2675	2675	2675	2675	2675	18000
14	**Savings/shortage**	100	1275	1275	1275	1275	1275	6475

Format the Numbers

To apply a specific format to numbers in your worksheet:

1 Select the cells that you wish to reformat, and click the arrow button in the bottom corner of the **Home** tab's [**Number**] group to open a dialog box providing options

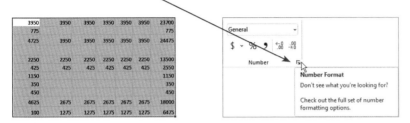

2 Click the **Number** tab, then choose the **Number** category

3 Select formatting options, such as: **Decimal places** 2, and **Negative numbers** "Red"

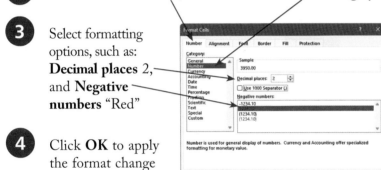

4 Click **OK** to apply the format change

5 Change the width of the columns to display all data (see page 27) and **Save** the changes

See pages 58-59 for details of the various types of formats available for numbers in cells.

Hot tip

Beware

The **General** format isn't consistent. Decimal places vary, and Excel may apply rounding to fit numbers in if the column is too narrow.

Print the Worksheet

1 Select the worksheet you want to print (if there's more than one in your workbook), click the **File** tab, then choose **Print** to open the print preview "Backstage" screen

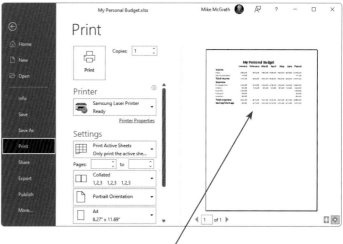

Hot tip

If you want to print only part of the data in the worksheet, select a range of cells before selecting **Print** (see the next page).

2 Check to see exactly what data will be printed, especially if there are more pages than you were expecting

3 To toggle between close-up and full-page view you can click the **Zoom to Page** button

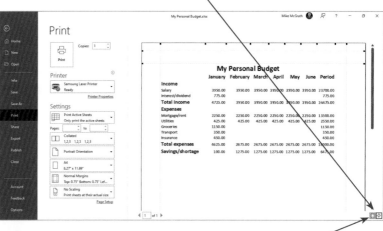

Beware

If you ever scroll past the end of the data and accidentally click a key or the spacebar, Excel will think this is part of the worksheet data.

4 You can also click the **Show Margins** button to toggle the margin indicators **On** or **Off**

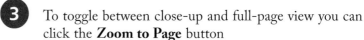

5 Click the **Printer** button to change the printer if desired

6 Click the **Settings** button to choose between the **Active Sheets**, the **Entire Workbook**, the current **Selection** or, if you don't want to limit the print, choose to simply **Ignore Print Area**

Other **Print** settings let you choose pages to print and to specify duplex, orientation, and paper size.

7 Specify the number of copies, then click the **Print** button to send the document to the printer

Excel will select a print area that will include all cells that appear to have data in them (including blanks), and as a result could select a larger print area than you might have anticipated. For printing part of the worksheet, you can preset the print area:

1 Select the range of cells that you want printed

2 Select the **Page Layout** tab, click the **Print Area** button in the [**Page Setup**] group, then select **Set Print Area**

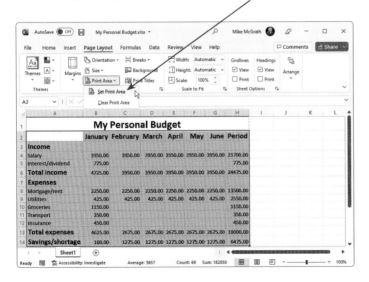

If you are sure that the default print settings are what you require, you can add the **Quick Print** button to the **Quick Access Toolbar** (see page 119) and use this to print immediately.

33

Insert, Copy, and Paste

You can rearrange the contents of the worksheet or add new data by inserting rows or columns and copying cells. For example, to add an additional six months of information:

1 Click in column **H**, press **Shift**, then click in column **M**

2 Select the **Home** tab, click the arrow next to **Insert** in the [**Cells**] group, and choose **Insert Sheet Columns**

3 Select **B2** and change the month name to "Jan", then autofill cells **C2:M2** with month names "Feb" to "Dec"

4 Select range **G4:G14**, then in the **Home** tab's [**Clipboard**] group click the **Copy** button

5 Select range **H4:M14,** and then click the **Paste** button in the **Home** tab's [**Clipboard**] group

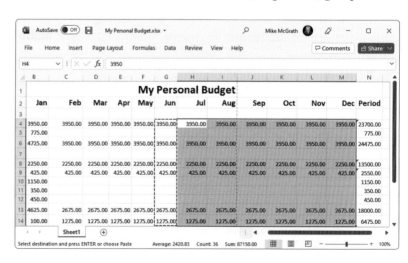

Hot tip

After copying the data range, change the formula in **N4** from **=SUM(B4:G4)** to **=SUM(B4:M4)**, and copy the formula into cells **N5:N6** and **N8:N14** to update all **Period** totals.

Period
47400.00
775.00
48175.00
0.00
27000.00
5100.00
1150.00
350.00
450.00
34050.00
14125.00

Excel Help

There are two ways to get help when using the Excel app – you can seek specific help using the **Search** box, or call upon the online **Help** facility for general assistance:

1 Click the **Search** box on the Title bar, then type the topic you want help with. For example, type "insert rows"

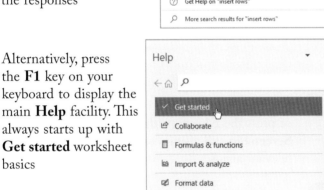

2 You'll see **Best Action**, other **Actions**, and further options. Review the most appropriate of the responses

3 Alternatively, press the **F1** key on your keyboard to display the main **Help** facility. This always starts up with **Get started** worksheet basics

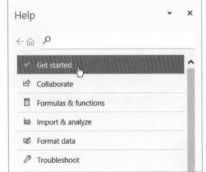

4 Select any entry to expand that topic and find links to subtopics

5 To get specific help on your chosen topic, type "insert rows" into the **Search** box then press **Return**

6 You'd get the same results if you selected **Get Help on "insert rows"** in the **Search** box results list

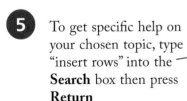

As well as online Help, **Search** uses **Smart Lookup**, which finds information on your search term from various online sources, including Wikipedia.

You can also access the Excel **Help** facility if you select the **Help** tab then click the **Help** icon.

Contextual Help

You do not always need to search for help – you can get specific information on a command or operation via a **ScreenTip**:

1 Open a command tab, then move the mouse pointer over a command in any of the groups to reveal a **ScreenTip**

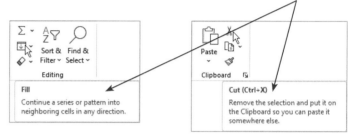

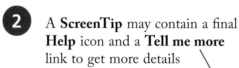

Fill

Continue a series or pattern into neighboring cells in any direction.

Cut (Ctrl+X)

Remove the selection and put it on the Clipboard so you can paste it somewhere else.

Don't forget

A **ScreenTip** may have just a brief description, plus a keyboard shortcut where appropriate. Or sometimes, a **ScreenTip** is more expansive.

2 A **ScreenTip** may contain a final **Help** icon and a **Tell me more** link to get more details

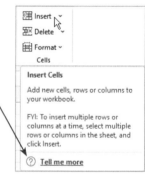

Insert
Delete
Format

Cells

Insert Cells

Add new cells, rows or columns to your workbook.

FYI: To insert multiple rows or columns at a time, select multiple rows or columns in the sheet, and click Insert.

? **Tell me more**

3 You can click the link or press the **F1** key (with the **ScreenTip** still visible) to see the relevant article

4 View the video, or scroll down to see more of the article

Hot tip

You can still use the **Search** box to locate additional articles on topics of interest.

Help

Search help

Insert or delete rows and columns

Insert and delete rows and columns to organize your worksheet better.

Choose Insert Sheet Row or Insert Sheet Column

Play

00:14 / 00:43

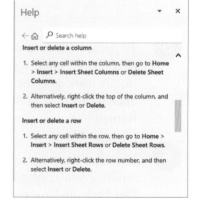

Help

Search help

Insert or delete a column

1. Select any cell within the column, then go to **Home > Insert > Insert Sheet Columns** or **Delete Sheet Columns**.

2. Alternatively, right-click the top of the column, and then select **Insert** or **Delete**.

Insert or delete a row

1. Select any cell within the row, then go to **Home > Insert > Insert Sheet Rows** or **Delete Sheet Rows**.

2. Alternatively, right-click the row number, and then select **Insert** or **Delete**.

Excel File Formats

When you save your workbook in Excel (see page 25) it uses the default file type **.xlsx**. To save your workbook in a format for old versions of Excel:

1 Click the **File** tab and select **Save As,** then browse to a preferred location (e.g. **Desktop**) by clicking the arrow button above the file name box

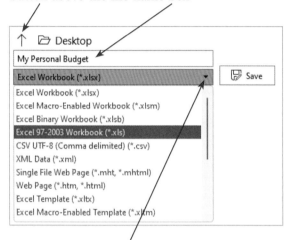

2 Click the drop-down arrow in the file type box (below the file name box) and select the **Excel 97–2003 Workbook (*.xls)** file type

3 Change the file name if desired, then click the **Save** button

4 You'll now see two copies of the workbook at your chosen location, with different file types and icons

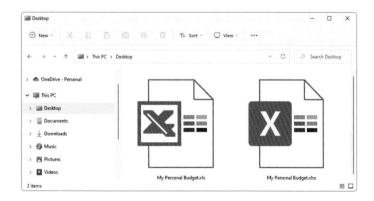

Hot tip

A workbook created in an earlier version of Excel will remain as file type **.xls** if modified – unless you choose to save it in modern **.xlsx** file format.

Don't forget

You can save and open files in the **Strict Open XML Spreadsheet (*.xlsx)** file format, which allows you to read and write ISO 8601 dates to resolve a leap-year issue for the year 1900 (see page 59).

Hot tip

The file icons indicate the specific file type, but to see the file extensions, select the **View** tab in File Explorer and click **Show**, **File name extensions**.

...cont'd

You can save your workbooks in a variety of other file formats, which will make it easier to share information with others who may not have the same applications. **Text (Tab delimited)** and **CSV (Comma delimited)** formats are often used to exchange information as most applications support these formats:

1 Click the **File** tab, select **Save As** and choose the format you want to use (e.g. **CSV**), then click the **Save** button

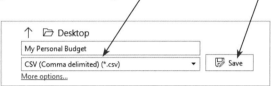

Hot tip

You can also display the **Save As** dialog by pressing the **F12** key.

2 You may be warned of potential conflicts. For example, you should use negative signs or brackets in numbers rather than the red font format seen in the **Format Cells** dialog on page 31, since colors are removed

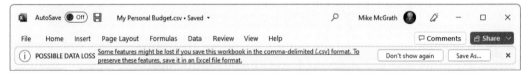

3 Text and number formatting will be removed, and only the current worksheet is saved

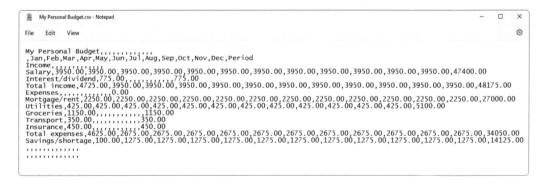

4 If there's more than one worksheet in your workbook, select and save each one in turn to a separate file

3 Manage Data

This chapter introduces navigation tools, commands, and facilities, to enable you to find your way around and work with large spreadsheets. It shows how existing data can be imported into Excel, to avoid having to retype information.

Use Existing Data

To identify the file types that can be opened directly in Excel:

1 Within a blank workbook/worksheet, select the **File** tab and click **Open** (or press **Ctrl + O**) and select the file location to launch the "Open" dialog

2 Click the file type box, alongside the **File name** box

3 Identify a file type supported by the other application (e.g. **Text Files**, **CSV**) then click **Cancel** for the moment

4 Extract data from the other application, as that file type

For example, you might have a number of MP3 tracks created by transferring your CD collection to the hard drive.

Each file stores details of the music it contains – title, album, artist, composer, recording date, bit-rate quality, genre, etc. This information is stored in the music file in the form of MP3 tags.

Hot tip

If the information you want to add to a workbook already exists in another application, you may be able to import it into Excel and use it without having to retype the data, as long as you can prepare it in a suitable file format.

...cont'd

Applications such as **Mp3tag (mp3tag.de/en/download.html)** can scan MP3 files and extract the tags, allowing you to make changes or corrections to the details that are saved.

1 Click **File**, **Change directory** to specify your **Music** folder

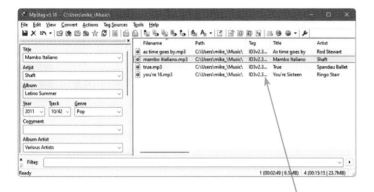

Details of the music are downloaded from the internet when you transfer tracks to the hard disk using an application like Windows Media Player. It also records the settings used for the conversion to MP3 format.

Mp3tag will scan all your music files and display the tag details.

2 Click **Edit**, **Select all files**, then **File**, **Export...** to launch an "Export" dialog

3 Choose the output file type (e.g. **CSV**) and click **OK** to output the tag details

4 In the next dialog, click **No** to avoid opening the **mp3tag.csv** file in Excel for the moment

5 Use **Notepad** to view the contents of the **CSV** file, which you will find in your **Music** folder

The first line gives field names for the selection of tags exported, and each subsequent line relates to one MP3 file with its values for each of the data fields.

41

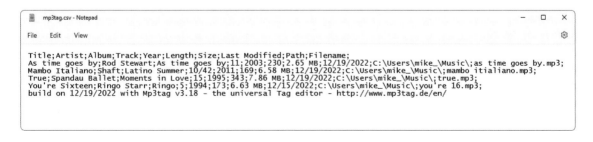

```
mp3tag.csv - Notepad                                                    —    □    ×

File   Edit   View                                                                ⚙

Title;Artist;Album;Track;Year;Length;Size;Last Modified;Path;Filename;
As time goes by;Rod Stewart;As time goes by;11;2003;230;2.65 MB;12/19/2022;C:\Users\mike_\Music\;as time goes by.mp3;
Mambo Italiano;Shaft;Latino Summer;10/42;2011;169;6.58 MB;12/19/2022;C:\Users\mike_\Music\;mambo itialiano.mp3;
True;Spandau Ballet;Moments in Love;15;1995;343;7.86 MB;12/19/2022;C:\Users\mike_\Music\;true.mp3;
You're Sixteen;Ringo Starr;Ringo;5;1994;173;6.63 MB;12/15/2022;C:\Users\mike_\Music\;you're 16.mp3;
build on 12/19/2022 with Mp3tag v3.18 - the universal Tag editor - http://www.mp3tag.de/en/
```

Import Data

1 Within Excel, select **Open** on the **File** tab, then **Browse** to select the data file you exported and click **Open**

Select the file type you used to export data from the application, and follow the prompts. This example shows the process for CSV text files.

2 This launches the "Text Import Wizard", which assesses your file and chooses appropriate settings – in this case, **Delimited**. Click the box to confirm your data has headers

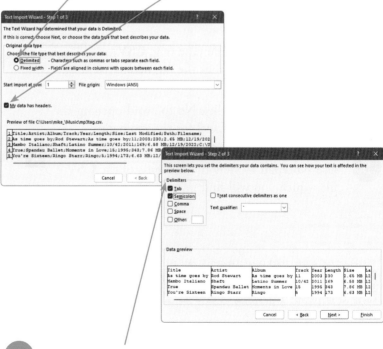

Check the settings applied by the import wizard, and make any changes that are required for your particular files.

3 Adjust the delimiters and the text qualifier for your file, if any changes are needed, and preview the effect

4 Review each column in turn and decide whether you want to skip that data item, change the data format, or accept the suggested format

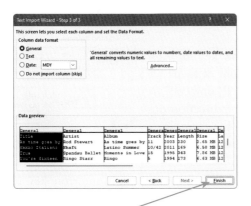

Hot tip

The **General** data format is the most flexible. It interprets numerical values as dates, leaving all other values as text.

5 Click the **Finish** button to load the data into your Excel worksheet, with lines as rows and data items as columns

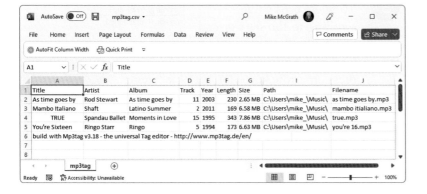

6 Select **Save As**, from the **File** tab, change the file type to "Excel Workbook", provide a name such as **Music-List** and press the **Save** button

Beware

Be sure to save the worksheet as **Excel Workbook**, not as a text file, and/or provide a new name to avoid the possibility of overwriting the original import file.

Navigate the Worksheet

If you've transferred information from an existing application and then find yourself with some rather large worksheets, you'll welcome the variety of ways Excel provides to move around the worksheet.

Arrow Keys

1 Press an arrow key to move the point of focus (the active cell) one cell per tap, in the direction of that arrow – for example, press the **Down** arrow key

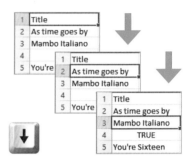

2 Hold down the **Ctrl** key and press an arrow key, to move to the start or end of a range of data (an adjacent set of occupied cells) – for example, press the **Ctrl** key and the **Right** arrow key

3 To select cells while scrolling to the start or end of a range, hold down the **Ctrl** and **Shift** keys and press an arrow key – for example, press **Ctrl + Shift** and the **Down** arrow key

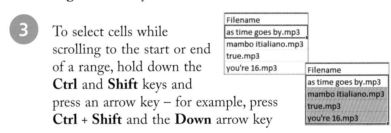

4 Press **Ctrl + Shift + arrow** again to extend the selection

Scroll Lock

Press **Scroll Lock** to turn on scroll locking. This changes the actions of the arrow keys.

1 The arrow keys move the window view up or down one row, or sideways one column, depending on which arrow key you use – for example, press the **Scroll Lock** key and the **Right** arrow key

2 The active cell is unchanged

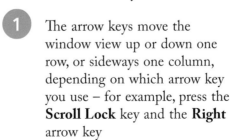

	A	B
1	Title	Artist
2	As time goes by	Rod Stewart
3	Mambo Italiano	Shaft
4	TRUE	Spandau Ballet
5	You're Sixteen	Ringo Starr

	B	C
1	Artist	Album
2	Rod Stewart	As time goes by
3	Shaft	Latino Summer
4	Spandau Ballet	Moments in Love
5	Ringo Starr	Ringo

Hot tip

Ctrl + arrow key takes you to the last occupied cell vertically, by the depth of the window, or horizontally, by the width of the window, depending on the arrow key you choose.

Don't forget

When **Scroll Lock** is selected, the words "Scroll Lock" are displayed on the status bar and, if present, the **Scroll Lock** light on the keyboard is turned on.

...cont'd

Scroll Bars

1 Click the vertical scroll arrows to move one row up or down

2 Click above or below the scroll box to move the view a window's depth up or down

3 Click the horizontal scroll arrows to move one column to the left or right, or click on the horizontal scroll bar to move the window width left or right

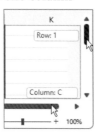

4 Click one of the scroll boxes. Excel displays the row number or column letter as you drag the scroll box

The sizes of the scroll boxes are based on the ratios of visible data to total data, and their positions are the relative vertical and horizontal locations of the visible area within the worksheet.

Split View

You can split the window so that you can scroll separate parts of the worksheet in two or four panes independently.

1 Select the cell where you want to apply the split, select the **View** tab and click **Split** in the [**Window**] group

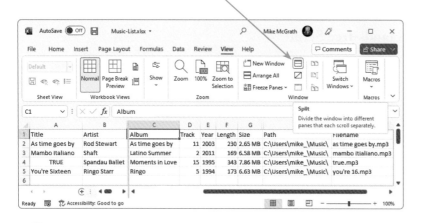

To reposition either the horizontal or vertical split divider, move the mouse pointer over the bar and drag using the double-headed arrow. To remove one or other divider, just double-click the bar.

2 The worksheet now has four panes with separate scroll bars

45

Scroll with the Mouse Wheel

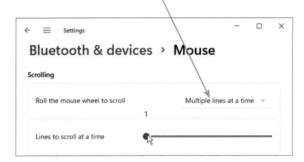

1 Rotate the wheel forward or back to scroll down or up a few lines at a time

2 To change the amount to scroll, open **Windows' Settings**, **Bluetooth & devices**, **Mouse** and change the number of lines, then select **Multiple lines** or **One screen** (at a time)

Hot tip

You can also open **Settings** and select **Bluetooth & devices**, **Mouse** to make adjustments to the way the mouse acts.

Continuous Scroll

1 Hold down the wheel button, then drag the pointer away from the origin mark, in the direction you want to scroll

2 Release the wheel when you reach the required position

Hands-free Scroll

1 To scroll automatically, click and release the wheel button, then move the mouse in the required direction

2 The further away from the origin mark you place the mouse pointer, the faster the scrolling

3 To slow down scrolling, move the mouse pointer back, closer to the origin mark

4 To stop automatic scrolling, click any mouse button

Hot tip

Move the pointer away from the origin mark to speed up scrolling. Move the pointer closer to the origin mark to slow down scrolling.

Keystrokes and Touch

The use of the arrow keys for navigation is covered on page 44. The Excel **Help** facility describes these additional keyboard shortcuts for a US keyboard layout (other layouts may differ):

End Key

- **End** – enter "End mode", then press one of the **Arrow** keys to move to the next non-blank cell in the same column or row as the active cell, and turn off "End mode".

- **Ctrl** + **End** – move to the last cell on the worksheet, the lowest used row of the rightmost used column.

- **Ctrl** + **Shift** + **End** – extend the selection to the last used cell on the worksheet (lower-right corner).

Home Key

- **Home** – move to the cell visible at the upper-left corner of the window.

- **Ctrl** + **Home** – move to the cell at the beginning of the worksheet.

- **Ctrl** + **Shift** + **Home** – extend the selection to the cell at the beginning of the worksheet.

Page Down Key

- **Page Down** – move one screen down in the worksheet.

- **Alt** + **Page Down** – move one screen to the right.

- **Ctrl** + **Page Down** – move to the next sheet in the workbook.

Page Up Key

- **Page Up** – move one screen up in the worksheet.

- **Alt** + **Page Up** – move one screen to the left.

- **Ctrl** + **Page Up** – move to the previous sheet in the workbook.

Tab Key

- **Tab** – move one cell to the right in the worksheet.

- **Shift** + **Tab** – move to the previous cell in the worksheet.

If you have a tablet PC or a touch-enabled monitor, you can easily scroll through the worksheet by dragging the screen horizontally or vertically.

Swipe the screen to move across the worksheet by a larger amount.

You can also use touch gestures to select ranges and autofill cells.

Display Excel **Help** (see page 35) for more information about using touch gestures in Excel.

Sort Rows

If you are looking for particular information, and don't know exactly where it appears in the worksheet, you can use Excel commands to help locate items.

1 Click the column containing the information, then from the **Home** tab's **[Editing]** group, select **Sort & Filter**

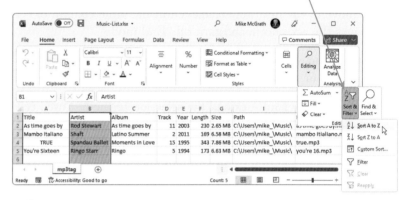

Custom Sort (see page 82) allows you to sort the worksheet by several fields – "Artists" and "Albums", for example.

2 Choose **Sort A to Z** (or choose **Sort Z to A** if the required information is toward the end of the list)

3 Choose **Expand the selection** to sort all columns (or **Continue with the current selection** to sort only the selected column), then click **Sort**

Excel provides a more structured way of handling a range of data like this, with the Excel Table – see pages 72-73.

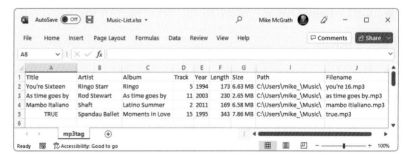

4 Scroll through the sorted list to find relevant entries, then click **Don't Save** when you close the workbook – to keep the original order

Find Entries

If you'd rather not change the sequence of rows, you can use the
Find command to locate appropriate entries.

1 Click the column with the
information, then choose
Find & Select from the
[**Editing**] group on the
Home tab, and click **Find...**
(or press **Ctrl + F**)

Don't
forget

Select all the cells in the
column – the search will
be restricted to that part
of the worksheet.

2 If necessary, click the
Options button (Excel remembers the last setting)

3 Specify a word
or phrase, then
select options
(e.g. **Find what:**
"summer" **Within:**
Sheet, Search: By
Columns, Look in:
Values, Find Next)

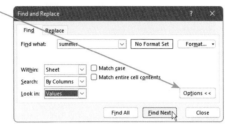

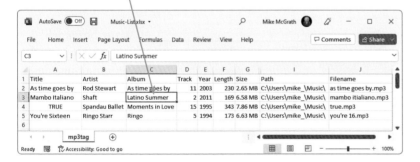

4 Keep selecting
Find Next,
to locate each
subsequent
matching entry,
or click **Find All**
to get a list of
the cell addresses
and values for all
matching entries

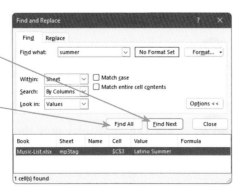

Hot tip

You can include case in
the check, and you can
require a full match with
the entire cell contents.

Filter Information

The **Filter** part of the **Sort & Filter** command can be very helpful in assessing the information you have imported, because it allows you to concentrate on particular sections of the data.

1 Select all the data (for example, click in the data region, press **Ctrl + End**, then press **Shift + Ctrl + Home**)

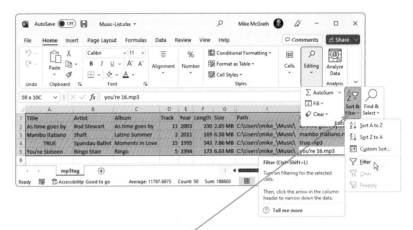

2 Select **Sort & Filter** from the **Home** tab's [**Editing**] group, then click the **Filter** command

Arrow boxes will now appear in each column alongside the headings.

3 Click the arrow box in any column heading to see a list of unique column values

4 Clear the boxes for unwanted values to leave those you want to view (e.g. favorite artists)

5 Click **OK** to display only those selected entries

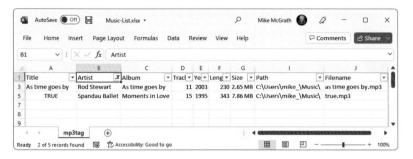

6 Make the changes that are required (e.g. select the "Artist" cells, then change the **Font** color to red)

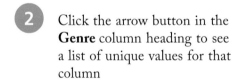

You can use **Filter** to assess the entries in your list. For example, to find those that have incomplete information:

1 Add a **Genre** column with just one "Rock/Pop" entry

2 Click the arrow button in the **Genre** column heading to see a list of unique values for that column

3 Filter for **Blanks** to see a list of entries that have no genre details so that you can update them as necessary

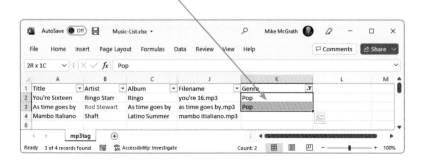

Having consistent values for entries makes it much easier to sort and organize your information.

To remove filters from all columns, reselect the **Filter** command from the **Home** tab, [**Editing**] group. All entries will then be displayed.

Remove Duplicate Entries

A duplicate entry is where all values in a row are an exact match for all the values in another row. To find and remove duplicates:

1 Copy and paste one row into a new row, to create a duplicate, then select the entire range of data cells

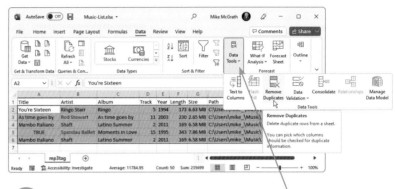

Hot tip

Sorting (see page 48) may help you spot repeated entries when data gets imported twice – but Excel offers a more systematic method.

2 Select the **Data** tab, then from the [**Data Tools**] group, click **Remove Duplicates**

3 Click **Select All** to ensure all columns are checked, then clear the boxes for some values if they may be repeated

Don't forget

Duplicate values are based on the displayed value, not on the stored value, so differences in format will make the entry appear unique.

4 Click **OK** to detect and delete duplicates – a message indicates how many duplicates were removed

Beware

There's no Undo option for this operation, so if you want to keep the original worksheet with the duplicates, save the revised version under a new name.

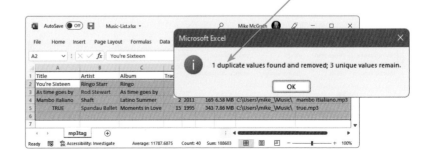

Check Spelling

A spelling check is sometimes a useful way to assess the contents of some sections of your worksheet.

1 Select the relevant parts. For example, click the **Title** column, press and hold **Ctrl**, then click the **Album** and **Genre** columns in turn

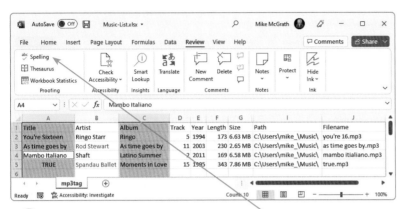

Select columns of data that contain text values that need spell-checking.

2 Select the **Review** tab, then click the **Spelling** command in the [**Proofing**] group, (or press **F7**) to launch a "Spelling" dialog

3 Click the **Change All** button if the word being corrected is likely to appear more than once in the list

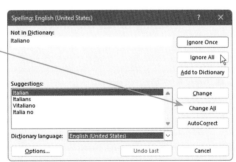

You can add foreign language dictionaries if they are required to spellcheck text in your worksheets. Click **File**, **Options**, **Language**, then under the **Office authoring languages and proofing** category click the **Add a language** button. Select a language to see it get added to the list box, then click the **Proofing available** link in the list box to install your selected language dictionary.

4 Click **Ignore All** if there are spelling warnings for valid terms or foreign words

5 Click **OK** when the check is completed and all required changes have been applied

53

Freeze Headers and Labels

When you navigate a worksheet, column headings and row labels will move off screen, making it more difficult to identify the data elements – but you can "freeze" these to keep them visible:

1 Select the **View** tab and click the **Freeze Panes** command, in the [**Window**] group

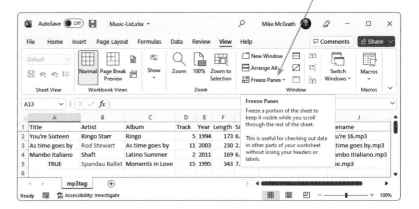

There are predefined options for a single heading row or a single label column.

2 Choose an option from the list. For example, choose **Freeze Top Row** to keep column headers visible when scrolling down the sheet

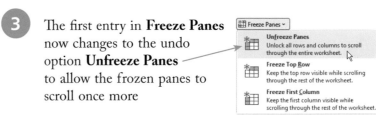

Beware

You cannot freeze rows and columns when you share your workbooks for collaborative changes.

3 The first entry in **Freeze Panes** now changes to the undo option **Unfreeze Panes** to allow the frozen panes to scroll once more

Hide Columns or Rows

To make it easier to view particular portions of the worksheet, you can tell Excel not to display certain columns or rows:

1 Select the columns or rows that you want to hide. To select non-adjacent columns, select the first column, hold down **Ctrl**, then select subsequent columns

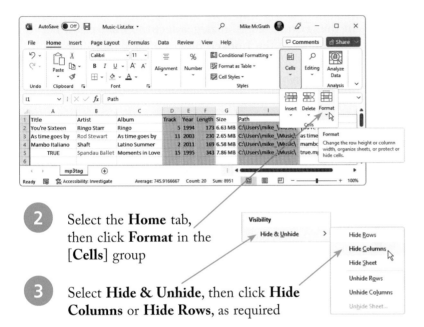

2 Select the **Home** tab, then click **Format** in the [**Cells**] group

3 Select **Hide & Unhide**, then click **Hide Columns** or **Hide Rows**, as required

To redisplay the hidden columns or hidden rows:

1 Select the columns either side of the hidden columns, or select the rows above and below the hidden rows

2 Open the **Hide & Unhide** menu and select **Unhide Columns** or **Unhide Rows**

You can also right-click a selected group of rows or columns, and then click **Hide** or **Unhide** from the context menu that appears.

You cannot cancel the selection of a cell or range of cells in a non-adjacent selection, without canceling the entire selection.

A column or row also becomes hidden if you change its column width or row height to zero. The **Unhide** command will reveal columns and rows hidden in this way.

Protect a Worksheet

1. Select any column (**Genre**, for example) that you might want to update

2. On the **Home** tab, select **Format** in the [**Cells**] group, then click **Format Cells...**

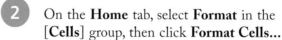

3. In the "Format Cells" dialog, select the **Protection** tab then uncheck the **Locked** box to unlock the column

Don't forget

Once you've set up your worksheet the way you want, you can lock it to protect it from being accidentally changed.

4. To protect the rest of the worksheet, select Excel's **Review** tab and click **Protect Sheet** in the [**Protect**] group

5. In the "Protect Sheet" dialog, check the options to ensure that all users are allowed to **Select locked cells** and to **Select unlocked cells**, then click **OK**

Beware

There's a greater need to protect workbooks in Excel if you use storage on OneDrive that is accessible to other users.

6. You can edit cells in the chosen columns (e.g. **Genre**), but you get an error message if you attempt to edit other cells (e.g. in the **Artist** column)

Hot tip

When you protect the sheet, the command changes to **Unprotect Sheet**, to allow you to reverse the process.

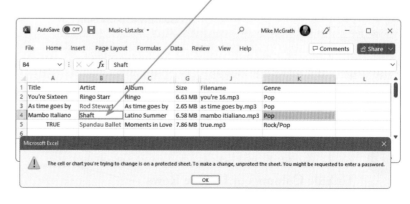

4 Formulas and Functions

Various formats for numbers are explained, and options for referencing cell locations are reviewed. These provide the basis for an introduction to functions and formulas, beginning with operators and calculation sequence, including formula errors and cell comments.

Number Formats

The cells in the worksheet contain values in the form of numbers or text characters. The associated cell formats control how the contents are displayed.

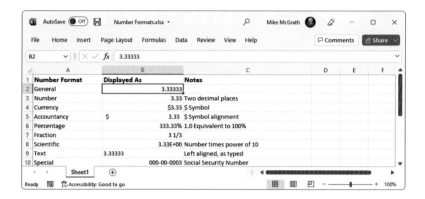

	A	B	C	D	E	F
1	Number Format	Displayed As	Notes			
2	General	3.33333				
3	Number	3.33	Two decimal places			
4	Currency	$3.33	$ Symbol			
5	Accountancy	$ 3.33	$ Symbol alignment			
6	Percentage	333.33%	1.0 Equivalent to 100%			
7	Fraction	3 1/3				
8	Scientific	3.33E+00	Number times power of 10			
9	Text	3.33333	Left aligned, as typed			
10	Special	000-00-0003	Social Security Number			

Cells **B2** to **B10** above all contain the same value (3.33333) but each cell has a different format, which changes the way the number appears on the worksheet. To set the number format:

1 Select a cell or cells, then click the **Home** tab and choose a format from the [**Number**] group, or click the arrow next to **Number** for more options

2 For greater control of the formats, such as how negative numbers appear, select **More Number Formats...** from the drop-down menu and choose a category and attributes from the **Format Cells** panel

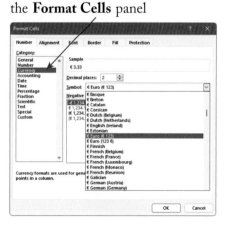

The default format is **General**, which is based on the cell contents. Use **Number** when you need decimal places, and **Currency** or **Accounting** for monetary values. The **Special** format is for structured numbers; e.g. zip or postal codes.

58

The values can be typed directly into the cells, imported from another application (see pages 42-43), or created by a formula.

...cont'd

Date and **Time** are also number formats, but in this case the number is taken as the days since a base point in time.

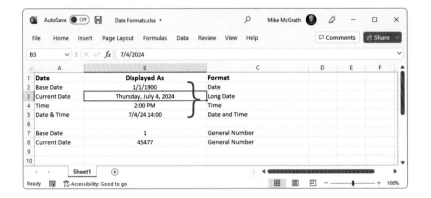

Because dates and times are stored as numbers, you can use them in formulas and calculations.

Cells **B2** to **B5** are formatted as **Date** or **Time**. The same dates in **B2** and **B3** are shown in cells **B7** and **B8**, formatted as **General Numbers**. This shows that day 1 is January 1st, 1900, while day 45477 is July 4th, 2024.

To set or change the date or time format:

1 Open **Format Cells**, select the **Number** tab, and click **Date** (or **Time**) to see a list of format options

Some of the formats depend on the specific country and locations defined in the Windows regional options, found in Windows' Settings.

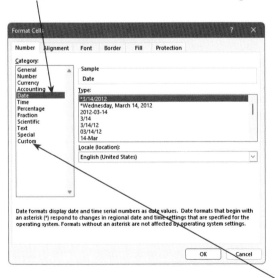

When dates are based on 1/1/1900, day 60 is incorrectly treated as February 29th, 1900. In Excel this can be resolved using the **Strict Open XML** file format (see page 37).

2 Choose a format option then click **OK**, or click **Custom** to see other time and date formatting options

Text Formats

Excel recognizes cells containing text, such as header and label cells, and gives them the **General** format, with default text format settings (left-aligned, and using the standard font). You can, however, view or change the format for such cells:

1. Select a cell or a range of cells, then click the bottom right-hand corner button on the [**Font**] group to open the **Format Cells** panel

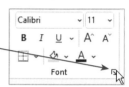

2. Select the **Font** tab to specify the font, style, size, and color, then click the **OK** button

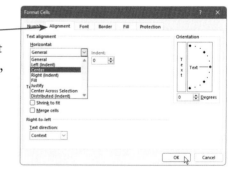

Hot tip

See page 30 for more examples on setting text format options for font and alignment, including the **Merge Cells** option.

3. Select the **Alignment** tab and specify the text controls, alignment, or orientation settings, then click the **OK** button

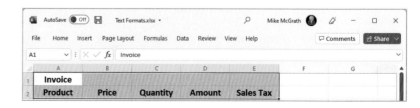

Relative References

A cell could contain a formula rather than an actual value. Excel performs the calculation the formula represents, and displays the result as the value for that cell. For example:

In this worksheet, cell **D3** shows the amount spent on "Gifts" (price times quantity), and is calculated as **=B3*C3**.

The formulas for **D4** and **D5** are created by copying and pasting **D3**. The cell references in the formula are relative to the position of the cell containing them, and are automatically updated for the new location.

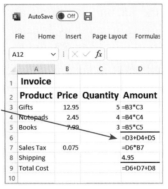

A cell reference in this form is known as a "relative reference", and this is the normal type of reference used in worksheets.

The results of formulas can be used in other formulas, so the total in cell **D6** is calculated as **=D3+D4+D5**.

Hot tip

Cells hold formulas as stored values, but it is the results that normally get displayed. To switch between results and formulas, press **Ctrl** + ` (the grave accent key), or select the **Formulas** tab and click **Show Formulas**.

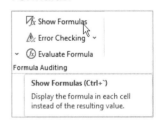

The sales tax in cell **D7** is calculated as **=D6*B7**. Note that **B7** is displayed as a value of 7.5%, the cell format being **Percentage**. The actual value stored in the cell is 0.075.

The worksheet could have used a constant value instead, such as **=D6*7.5/100** or **=D6*7.5%**. However, having the value stored in a cell makes it easier to adapt the worksheet when rates change. It also helps when the value is used more than once.

The shipping cost in cell **D8** is a stored constant.

The final calculation in the worksheet is the total cost in cell **D9**, which is calculated as **=D6+D7+D8**.

Don't forget

The value **B7** is a relative cell reference, like the others, but this may not be the best option. See page 62 for an alternative – an absolute cell reference.

Absolute References

Assume that calculation of the sales tax per line item is required. The value in cell **E3** for the "Gifts" product would be **=D3*B7**.

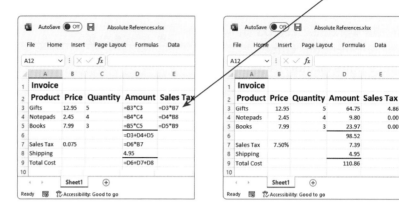

Don't forget

To fix a column, place **$** before the column letter. Likewise, to fix a row, put **$** before the row number. The other part of the reference will change when the formula is copied.

You might be tempted to copy this formula down into cells **E4** and **E5**, but, as you see above, the results would be incorrect, giving zero values, because the relative reference **B7** would be incremented to **B8** and then **B9** – both of which are empty cells. The answer is to fix the reference to **B7** so that it doesn't change when the formula is copied. To indicate this, edit the formula to place a **$** symbol in front of both the row and column addresses.

Hot tip

Select a cell reference in a formula and press F4 to cycle between relative, absolute, and mixed cell references – for example:

=B7
=$B$7
=B$7
=$B7

Copy this formula down into cells **E4** and **E5** and see that the reference **$B$7** doesn't change, so the results are correct. This form of cell reference is known as an "absolute reference". A cell reference with only part of the address fixed, such as **$D3** or **D$3**, would be known as a "mixed reference".

Name References

Names provide a different way to refer to cells in formulas. To create a name for a cell or cell range:

1 Select a cell or a group of cells you want to name

2 Click the **Name** box on the left of the Formula bar, then type the name you'll be using to refer to the selection and press **Enter**

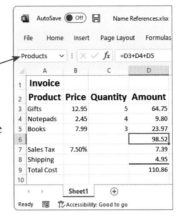

3 Click the **Formulas** tab and select **Define Name** in the [**Defined Names**] group to add additional named cells

4 Click the **Formulas** tab and select **Name Manager**, in the [**Defined Names**] group, to view names in the workbook

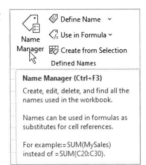

Names create absolute references to cells or ranges in the current worksheet. They can be used in formulas and, when these are copied, the references will not be incremented.

Don't forget

Names must start with a letter, an underscore, or a backslash. They can contain letters, numbers, periods/full stops, and underscores, but not spaces, and case is ignored. Their maximum length is 255 characters.

63

Hot tip

Names can be defined for a cell, for a range or group of cells, or for constants and functions.

Beware

You cannot use certain names, such as "R1", "R2", "R3", since these are actual cell references. You must specify non-ambiguous names, such as "Rate1", "Rate2", "Rate3", etc.

Operators

The formulas shown so far have used several operators (**+**, *****, **%**), but there are many other operators you might use, in a number of categories, including the following:

Operator	Meaning	Examples
Arithmetic		
+ (plus sign)	Addition	**A7+B5**
- (minus sign)	Subtraction Negation	**C6-20** **-C3**
* (asterisk)	Multiplication	**C5*C6**
/ (forward slash)	Division	**C6/D3**
% (percent sign)	Percent	**20%**
^ (caret)	Exponentiation or Power	**D3^2**
Comparison		
= (equal)	Equal to	**A1=B1**
> (greater than)	Greater than	**A1>B1**
< (less than)	Less than	**A1<B1**
>= (greater than with equal sign)	Greater than or equal	**A1>=B1**
<= (less than with equal sign)	Less than or equal	**A1<=B1**
<> (not equal)	Not equal	**A1<>B1**
Text		
& (ampersand)	Connect/join	**"ABCDE"&"FGHI"**
Reference		
: (colon)	Range	**B5:B15**
, (comma)	Union	**SUM(B5:B15,D5:D15)**
(space)	Intersection	**B2:D6 C4:F8**

Don't forget

Operators can be applied to constants, cell references, or functions.

Don't forget

The results of any of these comparisons will be a logical value – either True or False.

Hot tip

The intersection of two ranges is a reference to all cells that are common between the two ranges.

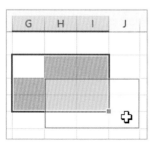

Calculation Sequence

The order in which a calculation is performed may affect the result. As an example, the calculation **6+4*2** could be interpreted in two different ways. If the addition is performed first, this would give **10*2**, which equals 20. However, if the multiplication is performed first, the calculation becomes **6+8**, which equals 14.

To avoid any ambiguity in calculations, Excel evaluates formulas by applying operators in a specific order. This is known as "operator precedence". The top-to-bottom sequence is as follows:

Don't forget

Operator precedence is a mathematical concept used by all programming languages and applications, such as spreadsheet programs that include computation.

1	: ,	Colon Space Comma
2	-	Negation
3	%	Percentage
4	^	Exponential
5	* /	Multiplication Division
6	+ -	Addition Subtraction
7	&	Concatenation
8	= < > <= >= <>	Comparison

When a formula has several operators with the same precedence such as * multiplication and / division, Excel evaluates the operators from left to right.

These are some example formulas that illustrate the effect of operator precedence on the calculation result:

Beware

Operator precedence in Excel is not always the same as mathematical precedence. For example, take the expression **-3²**. This is entered as **-3^2**, which Excel evaluates as **(-3)^2**, which is +9. However, mathematically, you'd expect **-(3^2)**, which is -9.

	A	B	C
1	=4+6*3	22	Multiply, then Add
2	=(4+6)*3	30	Add in parentheses, then Multiply
3	=4+6/2*3	13	Divide, then Multiply, then Add
4	=(4+6)/(2*3)	1.6667	Multiply, then Add, then Divide
5	=((4+6)/2)*3	15	Add, then Divide, then Multiply
6			

7	=3^2	9
8	=(-3)^2	9
9	=-(3^2)	-9

You use parentheses to change the order of evaluation, since the expressions within parentheses are evaluated first. If there are parentheses within parentheses, Excel evaluates the expression in the innermost pair of parentheses first, then works outward.

Functions

Functions are predefined formulas that perform calculations based on specific values, called arguments, provided in the required sequence. A function begins with the function name, followed by an opening parenthesis, the arguments for the function separated by commas, and a closing parenthesis. They are used for many types of calculations, ranging from simple to highly complex.

If you are unsure which function is appropriate for a task, Excel will help you search for the most appropriate. To select a function in the example Invoice worksheet:

Arguments can be numbers, text, cell references, or Boolean values (True or False).

1 Click the cell where you want to use a function as the formula – the total amount cell **D6**, for example

2 Click **Formulas**, [**Function Library**], **Insert Function** on the Ribbon to open a dialog

3 Enter the phrase "add numbers" in the **Search for a function** box, and click **Go** to list related functions

4 Select the appropriate function – in this case, **SUM** – and click **OK**

Several Excel functions can be found in the various categories offered on page 88.

5 Review the arguments suggested – in this case, range **D3:D5** – and see the answer this gives. Adjust the range if needed, then click **OK** to insert the function

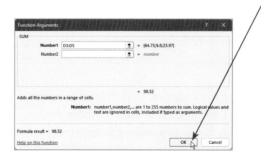

66

...cont'd

AutoComplete

Even when you know the function needed, Excel will help you set it up, to help avoid possible syntax and typing errors:

1 Click the worksheet cell, and begin typing the function. For example, click the total cost cell **D9** and type **=s**

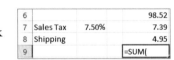

2 Excel lists functions that match so far so that you can select a function and see its description. Scroll down to see more names, or continue typing. For example, type **=su** to narrow down the list

Hot tip

Click on the function name in the drop-down list, to display a ScreenTip describing that function.

3 When you find the function that you require, double-click the name, then enter the arguments that are shown

6			98.52
7	Sales Tax	7.50%	7.39
8	Shipping		4.95
9			=SUM(

4 For example, click **D6**, press : colon, then click **D8**

6			98.52
7	Sales Tax	7.50%	7.39
8	Shipping		4.95
9			=SUM(D6:D8)

5 Type the closing parenthesis, then press **Enter**

Don't forget

Type the range name, if you have already defined the required cells (see page 63).

6 The formula with the function is stored in the cell, and the result of the chosen operation gets displayed

6			98.52
7	Sales Tax	7.50%	7.39
8	Shipping		4.95
9			110.86

As always, you should save the spreadsheet from time to time, to preserve your changes.

AutoSum

1 Select a cell below a column of numbers

	A	B	C	D	E
1	1	5	9	18	
2					
3	4				
4	8				
5	16				
6	32				
7					

2 Now, click **Σ AutoSum**, in the **Home** tab's [**Editing**] group

Σ AZ Y O
Sort & Find &
Filter Select
Editing

Sum (Alt+=)
Automatically add it up. Your total will appear after the selected cells.

All the cells up or across, to the first non-numeric or empty cell, are included in the total.

3 Press **Enter**, or click on the check mark in the **Formula bar**, to add the function to total the column selection

SUM ✕ ✓ *fx* =SUM(A3:A6)

	A	B	C	D	E
1	1	5	9	18	
2					
3	4				
4	8				
5	16				
6	32				
7	=SUM(A3:A6)				
8	SUM(**number1**, [number2], ...)				

In either case, you can click the arrow next to **AutoSum** and select from the list of functions offered to apply a different function to the range of values.

4 Similarly, select the cell to the right of a row of numbers and click **AutoSum** to total the row

SUM ✕ ✓ *fx* =SUM(A1:D1)

	A	B	C	D	E
1	1	5	9	=SUM(A1:D1)	
2					SUM(**number**
3	4				
4	8				
5	16				
6	32				
7	60				

When the selected cell could be associated with a row or a column, **AutoSum** will usually favor the column. However, you can adjust the direction or extent of the range in the formula before you apply it to the worksheet.

The **AutoSum** function can also be found in the [**Function Library**] group, on the **Formulas** tab, along with **Insert Function**, **Recently Used**, and various other functions – such as **Financial**, **Logical**, and **Text**.

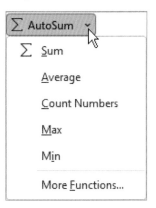

Σ AutoSum ˅
Σ Sum
Average
Count Numbers
Max
Min
More Functions...

fx Σ AutoSum ˅ ⬚ Logical ˅
Insert Recently Used ˅ A Text ˅
Function Financial ˅ Date & Time ˅
Function Library

Formula Errors

Excel helps you to avoid some of the more common errors when you are entering a formula:

1 When you type a name, Excel outlines the associated cell or range so that you can confirm that it is the correct selection

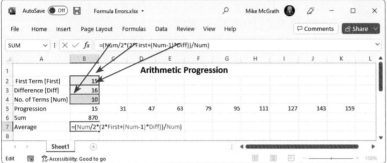

$$(Num/2*(2*First+(Num-1)*Diff)) /Num$$

2 With nested functions, Excel colors the cell names and also the parentheses to help you ensure that they are in matching open/close pairs

3 If you do make an error, such as the extra parenthesis shown above, it is often detected and corrected

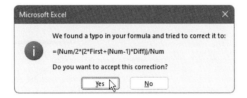

4 If the cell content overflows the cell size, Excel displays **#** hash signs within the cell

5 Other errors additionally display a green flash at the top-left corner of the cell

6 Select the cell, then click the information icon for details and options for dealing with the problem

In this example, **First**, **Diff**, and **Num** are defined names.

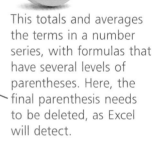
Hot tip

This totals and averages the terms in a number series, with formulas that have several levels of parentheses. Here, the final parenthesis needs to be deleted, as Excel will detect.

69

Don't forget

Common errors include **#REF!** (invalid reference), **#VALUE!** (invalid value), **#NAME?** (invalid name).

Add Notes

You can add Notes to a cell, perhaps to explain the way in which a particular formula operates:

1 Click the cell where the **Note** is meant to appear

2 Select the **Review** tab, and click **New Note**, in the [**Notes**] group

3 A dialog appears containing your username and a text box in which you can type a **Note**

4 Format text in the **Note** as desired, then click outside the **Note** box when you've finished the **Note**

Hot tip

When there are Notes in your worksheets, you can print them as displayed on the sheet, or at the end of the sheet.

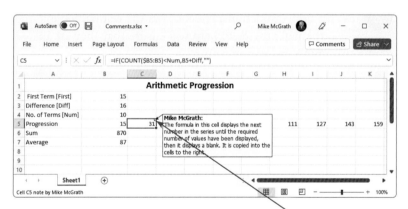

5 The presence of a **Note** is indicated by a red flash at the top-right corner of the cell, and the **Note** box appears when you move the mouse over the cell

6 To delete a **Note**, select the **Review** tab and click the **Delete** icon in the [**Comments**] group

Beware

Notes was previously called "Comments", but now Comments are threaded and allow you to have discussions with other people. **Notes** now work like Comments used to work for adding annotations in earlier versions of Excel.

5 Excel Tables

The Excel Table structure helps you to keep sets of data separate so that you don't accidentally change other data when you are inserting or deleting rows and columns. There are other benefits also, such as structured cell references, automatic filters, sorts, and subtotals.

Create an Excel Table

To make it easier to manage and analyze a group of related data, you can turn a range of cells into an Excel **Table**. The range should contain no empty rows or empty columns. To illustrate this feature, a table is used to interpret the genre (music classification) codes contained in the MP3 tags for music files (see pages 40-41). This field often appears as a genre code such as (2) for "Country music" or (4) for "Disco". Search on the internet for "ID3 genre code table", and select a suitable web page – for example, at:
gnu.org.ua/software/idest/manual/html_section/Genre-Codes. html

1 Select the code table in your browser, then press **Ctrl + C**

2 Open the **Music.xlsx** file's worksheet, and type "GenreID#" and "Genre" headers in two empty columns

3 Select the second cell in the first of those columns, then press **Ctrl + V** to copy the code table into the worksheet

Hot tip

In an Excel Table, the rows and columns are managed independently from the data in other rows and columns on the worksheet. In earlier releases of Excel, this feature was called an Excel List.

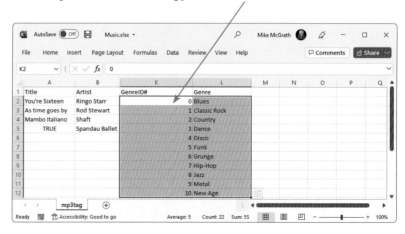

4 With the data <u>and</u> headers selected, click the **Insert** tab, then click **Table** in the [**Tables**] group

It may be best to remove worksheet protection and unfreeze panes before you insert the new data.

5 Check that the appropriate range of data is selected

6 If the first row has headers, check **My table has headers** – otherwise, you'd let Excel generate default headers

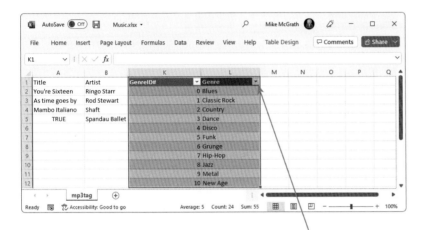

If you click in the table, the context-sensitive **Table Design** tab is displayed so that you can customize or edit the table settings.

73

The table is given the default banding style, and **Filter** buttons are automatically added in the header row of each column, allowing you to sort or filter the contents. The table will be given a default name, such as "Table1". To change this name:

1 Select the table, and click the added **Table Design** tab

2 Click the **Table Name** box in the [**Properties**] group, to highlight the name

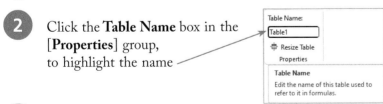

3 Type a new name for the table – e.g. "Code" – and press **Enter** to apply the change (and update all references to the old table name)

You can also change the names of tables, using the **Name Manager** on the **Formulas** tab (see page 63).

Edit Tables

1 Select the music data and click **Insert**, [**Tables**], **Table** to create another table, and change its name to "Tunes"

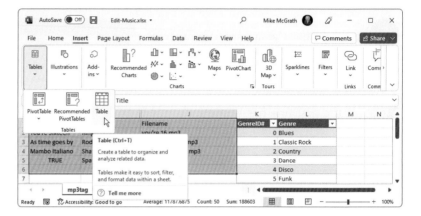

Hot tip

You can insert more than one table in the same worksheet, and work with each of them independently. Inserting or deleting rows or columns in one table will not affect other tables.

2 Click any unrequired columns in the new "Tunes" table, then select **Home** and click **Delete** in the [**Cells**] group

3 Click in the last cell of the "Code" table, and press **Tab** – to add a row

4 Type an entry, such as "11", "Salsa", then add a row with "12", "Unknown"

Don't forget

Click adjacent cells to delete more than one column or row in the table at a time.

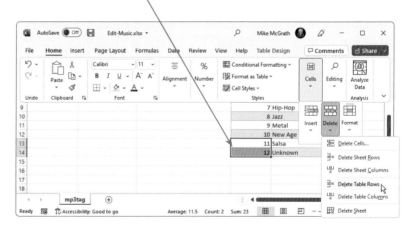

5 Select the cells with values 11 and 12, then select **Home**, [**Cells**], **Delete**, **Delete Table Rows**

Table Styles

The **Table Design** tab provides options to change the formatting of rows and columns in a table.

1 Specify if there's a header row, and turn banding on or off, using settings in the [**Table Style Options**] group

Styles are grouped into light, medium, and dark sets, with additional effects for end columns, and for banding.

2 Click the **Quick Styles** button, in the [**Table Styles**] group, to view a full list of styles

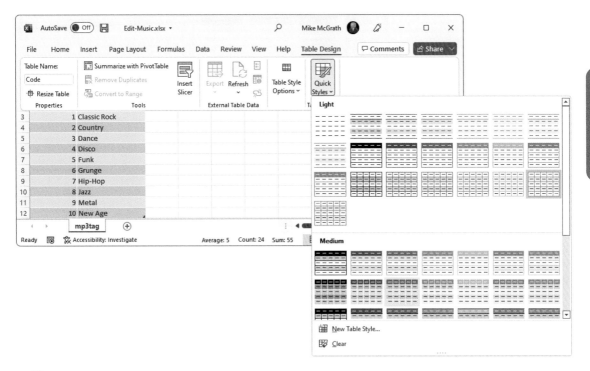

3 Move the mouse pointer over a style option, and see the table preview the effects that would apply

4 Click on a style option to apply that style to your table

Table Totals

You can add a **Total Row** at the end of the table to display the totals for columns (or use another function appropriate to the type of information stored in the column). To add table totals:

① Select the table, click the **Table Design** tab, and check the **Total Row** box in the **[Table Style Options]** group

The **Subtotal** function is inserted, with a number to indicate the operation:

101	Average
102	Count
103	Counta
104	Max
105	Min
106	Product
107	Stdev
108	Stdevp
109	Sum
110	Var
111	Varp

Subtotal uses structured references for the table (see page 78).

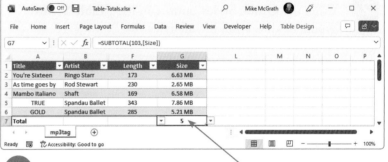

② A **Total Row** gets added at the end of the table, and the last column displays a value – here, it's the number of tracks

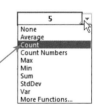

③ Select the total number cell, and click the drop-down button to see the function applied – in this case, it's **Count**, which counts non-blank cells in the column

④ You can apply a total to any column – for example, for "Length" you could choose the **Sum** function

The **More Functions...** drop-down menu option allows any Excel function to be used to compute the total for that column.

Count Unique Entries

You may sometimes want to discover how many unique entries are contained within a range of data where duplicates might exist. For example, in an "Artist" column, you can count all unique entries, to give the numbers of individual artists stored in the table:

1 Click in the **Total** cell for the "Artist" column, and begin typing the function **=sum(1/countif(**

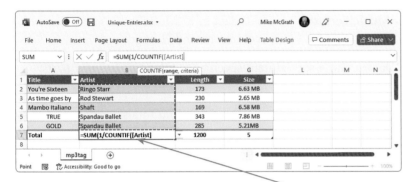

77

Beware

This method of counting the number of duplicate entries assumes there are no empty cells in the range being checked.

2 Select the range of cells to be examined to see **[Artist]** get added to the function

3 Type a comma in the function, then select the range again to add a second **[Artist]** instance to the function

4 Type two closing parentheses to complete the function

5 Press **Enter** and the count of unique entries within the range will be displayed

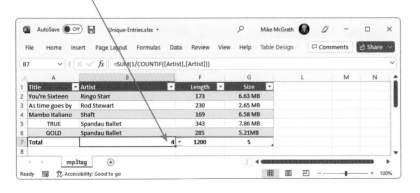

Hot tip

This function calculates the frequency for each entry, inverts these counts, and sums up the resulting fractions. For example, if an entry appears three times, you get 1/3 + 1/3 + 1/3 for that entry, giving a count of 1. Each unique entry adds another 1.

Structured References

The formulas shown for totals illustrate the use of structured references. These allow you to refer to the contents of a table using meaningful names, without having to be concerned about specific row numbers and column letters, or changes that are caused when rows and columns are added or deleted. The structured references use the table name and column specifiers:

=Music	All data in a table named "Music".
=Music[Length]	All data in a "Music" table's column named "Length".

You can add a special item specifier to refer to particular parts:

=Music[#All]	The entire "Music" table, including headers, data, and totals.
=Music[#Data]	All data in a "Music" table.
=Music[#Headers]	The header row of a "Music" table.
=Music[#Totals]	The **Total Row** of a "Music" table.
=[@Length]	The intersection of a "Length" column with the active row cell.

Formulas within the table, such as subtotals on the **Total Row**, can leave off the table name. This forms an unqualified structured reference (e.g. **[Filename]**). However, outside the table, you need the fully-qualified structured reference (e.g. **Music[Filename]**).

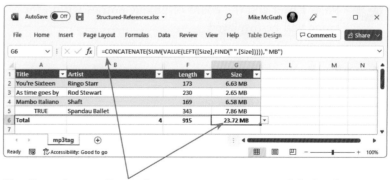

The formula in cell **G6** above contains two unqualified references to the "Size" column. It separates the numeric values from the "MB" text by finding a single space within each cell to display the total file size of all tracks, then adds " MB" to the total size.

The use of structured references in formulas is more efficient than using full column references (e.g. **$F:$F**), dynamic ranges, or arrays.

Earlier versions of Excel referenced this intersection as **Music [[#This Row],[Length]]**, but it's now simplified to **[@Length]**.

78

You should avoid the use of special characters such as a space, tab, line feed, comma, colon, period/full stop, bracket, quote mark, or an ampersand in your table and column names.

Calculated Columns

You can add a calculated column to an Excel Table. This uses a single formula that adjusts for each row, automatically expanding to include additional rows.

Start by inserting a new column in a table:

1 Click the far right column of a table, then select the **Home** tab, and click the arrow next to **Insert** – located in the [**Cells**] group

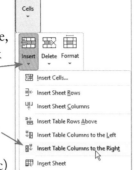

2 Click **Insert Table Columns to the Right**, and then rename the new column as "Style" (i.e. style of music)

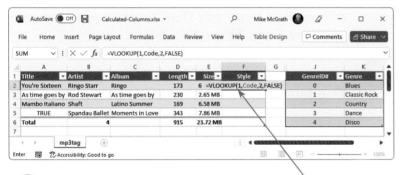

3 Click anywhere in the Style column and type a formula – e.g. **=VLOOKUP(1,Code,2,FALSE)** – then press **Enter** to update the cells in the column

4 The formula is automatically filled in to all the cells in the column, above as well as below the active cell

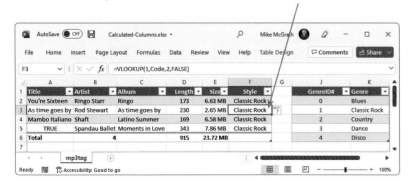

You need to enter the formula only once, and you won't need to use the **Fill** or **Copy** command when the table grows.

The **VLOOKUP** formula in this example is a vertical table lookup. It matches the value 1, in the first column of the **Code** table (the GenreID#). It then copies the associated value on that row in the second column of the **Code** table (Genre) into the Style column. There is also an **HLOOKUP** function to perform a horizontal lookup.

Insert Rows

1 Scroll to the last cell in the table, press **Tab** to add a new row, and you'll see that the new formula is replicated

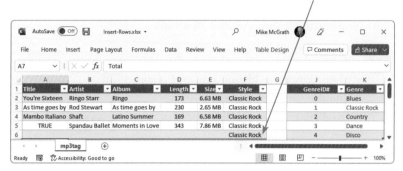

2 To add data from a text file (see pages 42-43), click a cell in an empty part of the worksheet, then select **Data**, [**Get & Transform Data**], **Get Data, From File** on the menu, and **From Text/CSV** on the submenu

3 Locate and double-click the data file, and use the **Transform Data** feature to modify its structure if required

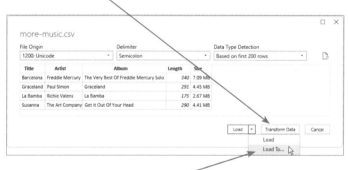

4 Select **Load, Load To...** and choose **Table, New worksheet** to add the data to the temporary location

5 Click **OK** to load the data into the new worksheet that will appear on a separate worksheet tab named "more-music" – as is the CSV file name

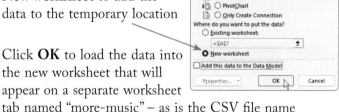

Beware

Adding empty rows may cause temporary errors in formulas that need data in all cells, as illustrated here. The problems will be resolved as soon as data gets added.

Hot tip

You cannot import data directly from an external source into the table, so you must use another worksheet or another part of the current worksheet as an interim.

6 Highlight the new data (excluding the header row), then select the **Home** tab and click [**Clipboard**], **Copy**

Hot tip

You can type new rows directly into the table, pressing **Tab** at the end of each row, ready to enter the next row.

7 Select the first cell in the row added to the table on the first worksheet, and click **Home**, [**Clipboard**], **Paste**

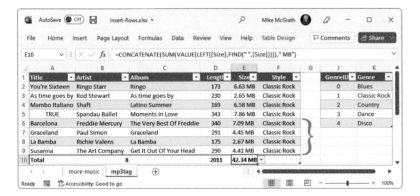

8 Additional rows are put into the table as necessary, and the data records are copied into those new rows

9 You'll see that totals are updated and Style (the calculated column) displays the associated values for the new entries

10 Right-click the second worksheet tab, then select **Delete** to remove the temporary location for the additional data

Beware

Adding new rows or columns to the table causes worksheet data outside the table to be shifted. You should check for potential problems in data that is not in a defined table.

Custom Sort

When new rows are inserted, it may be appropriate to sort the table to position the new rows where they belong.

To do this:

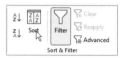

1 Click in the table, select the **Home** tab, click **Sort & Filter** in the [**Editing**] group, and select **Custom Sort...**

Or

Click in the table, select the **Data** tab, and click **Sort**, in the [**Sort & Filter**] group

Don't forget

By default, columns with text values are sorted A to Z, while columns with number values are sorted smallest to largest.

2 The first time there are no criteria defined, so click the arrow button in **Sort by** to add a header (e.g. Artist)

Hot tip

The sorting criteria used for each table will be saved when the workbook is saved, so it is easy to re-sort in the same way, after future updates and modifications. The **Filter** button icon for relevant columns is modified to show sorting is in effect.

3 Click the **Add Level** button and choose a second header (e.g. Title), then click **OK** to apply the sort sequence

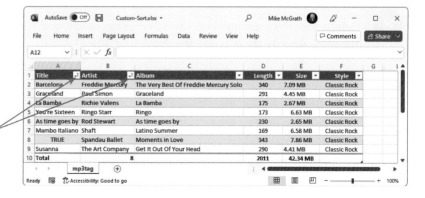

Print a Table

You can print a table without having to select the print area specifically (see pages 32-33):

1 Use **Filters** to restrict the data to print – e.g. **Artist**, **Text Filters**, **Begins With...** – to open a "Custom Autofilter" dialog

2 Then, type "R" to select only artists whose name begins with the letter R

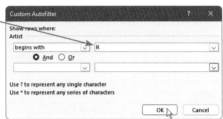

3 Press the **File** tab, then select **Print** (or press **Ctrl + P**) to open the Backstage "Print" screen

4 For **Settings**, choose **Print Selected Table**, then adjust the paper size and scaling if needed

5 Specify the number of copies required, then click the **Print** button to complete the process by sending your selection to a printer

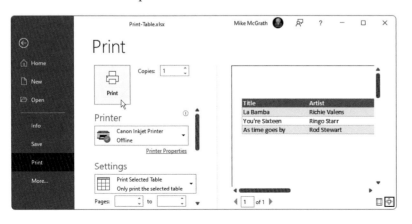

You may wish to change to a different table style – one more suitable for printing (or select **None** for a plain effect).

Some formulas on a Total Row, if present, may continue to reference the whole of the table contents.

You can print the active worksheet, the entire workbook, the selected data, or the active table.

Summarize a Table

You can summarize data using the **PivotTable** feature. See page 165 for another example.

1 Click in the table, select the **Insert** tab, then in the [**Tables**] group click **PivotTable**, then select **From Table/Range**

2 Choose a location for the **PivotTable** report – either a new worksheet or an empty portion of the current worksheet – then click **OK**

3 An empty **PivotTable** report appears at the specified location, and a "PivotTable Fields" panel appears where you can select and arrange fields to be included

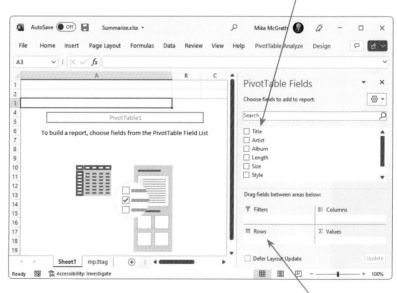

4 By default, text fields are added to the **Rows** area, and fields containing numbers are added to the **Values** area, when you check the boxes to select fields from the list (for example, **Title**, **Artist**, and **Length**)

5 You can rearrange the fields by dragging between areas, or arranging the items in each field in a different order to change their prominence

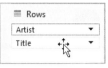

6 Click a numeric field in the **Values** list to reposition, move to a different area, or remove the field

7 Click **Value Field Settings...** to open a dialog where you can choose a **Custom Name** for the field

When you click a field name that has text values, and then select **Field Settings**, it will display appropriate text options for that field.

8 Choose how you wish to summarize the values (**Sum**, **Count**, **Average**, **Min**, **Max**, etc.) then click **OK** to close the dialog and see the **PivotTable** report

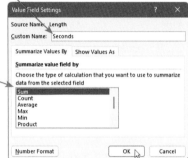

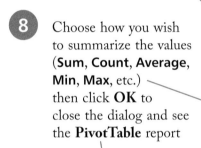

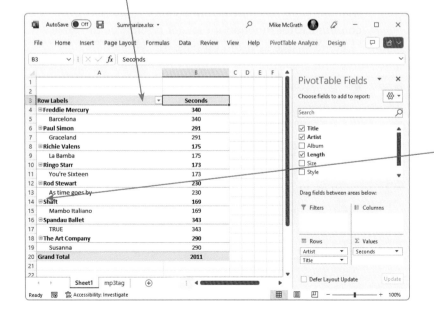

Fields containing sub-fields have buttons to expand or collapse their sub-fields. **PivotTable Analyze** and **Design** tabs are added to the Ribbon. Select **+/- Buttons** in the **PivotTable Analyze**, [**Show**] group to show or hide these buttons.

Convert to a Range

You can turn an Excel Table back into a range of data:

Hot tip

If you have just created a table from a range of data (see pages 72-73), you can switch back to the range format by clicking **Undo** on the **Home** tab's [**Undo**] group.

Don't forget

To remove the table style from the cells, select all the data, click the **Home** tab, click the Down arrow next to **Cell Styles** in the [**Styles**] group, and choose the **Normal** style.

Beware

To convert the range back into a table you would have to recreate formulas for the **Total Row**.

1 Click in the table, then select the **Table Design** tab and click **Convert to Range** in the [**Tools**] group

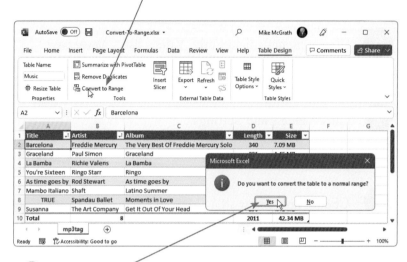

2 Click **Yes** to confirm that you do want to convert the table to a data range, and see the cell styles preserved but the filter boxes get removed from the header cells

3 The **Total Row** values still appear, but all references are now standard absolute cell references – the "Length" column's **Total** function no longer references the table "Length" name as it did on page 76

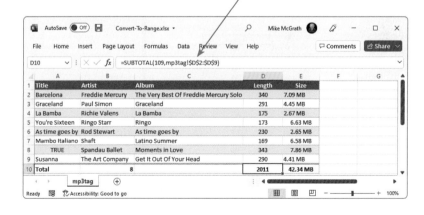

6 Advanced Functions

There is a large library of Excel functions available. To help locate the ones you want, related functions are grouped by category, and there's a Recently Used list. More functions are provided via Excel Add-ins. With nested functions in your formulas, use the Evaluate command to see how they work.

Function Library

1 Select the **Formulas** tab to see the [**Function Library**] group, with a Ribbon style that depends on your current window size

Hot tip

Select **More Functions** from the [**Function Library**] group for other categories – including **Statistical**, **Engineering** and **Web**.

The *fx* **Insert Function** command, on the left of the group, will allow you to enter keywords to **Search for a function** (see page 66). It provides the syntax and a brief description for any function that you select, plus a link to more detailed help. Alternatively, you can select from one of the categories.

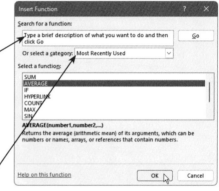

2 Click any of the category entries for an alphabetical list of the names of the functions that it includes. The categories and the number of functions included in each are:

Most Recently Used	10	**Text**	28
All	459	**Logical**	11
Financial	55	**Information**	20
Date & Time	24	**Engineering**	54
Math & Trig	74	**Cube**	7
Statistical	110	**Compatibility**	42
Lookup & Reference	19	**Web**	3
Database	12		

All – provides an alphabetical list from **ABS** to **ZTEST** of every function included in Excel, giving you a way to search for a function when you have no idea which category it belongs to.

Most Recently Used – remembers the functions you last used, allowing you to make repeated use of functions with the minimum of fuss, without needing their particular categories.

Hot tip

The [**Function Library**] group continues to expand as Excel continues to evolve.

Logical Functions

Sometimes the value for one cell depends on the value in another cell. For example, test scores could be used to set grade levels.

1 The formula in **C2** is **=B2>=50** and gives the result True or False, depending on the value that is in **B2**

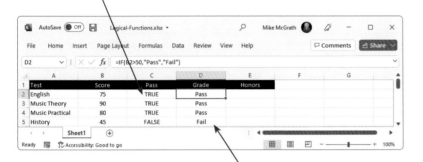

2 To display more meaningful results you can use an **IF** formula, such as **=IF(B2>=50,"Pass","Fail")**

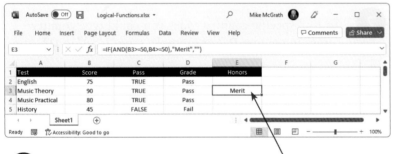

3 Sometimes you need to check two conditions, such as the formula **=IF(AND(B3>=50,B4>=50),"Merit","")**

IF functions can be nested, where a FALSE return is replaced by another **IF** function to make another test, such as the formula below:

Hot tip

Comparison operators
< (less than),
= (equal to), and
> (greater than) form
expressions that compare
two values and return
a TRUE or FALSE result.
The **IF** function evaluates
the result of a given
expression and performs
an appropriate action.

Hot tip

Comparison operators
can be combined as
<= (less or equal to),
>= (greater or equal to).
The **AND** function
includes multiple
comparison expressions,
which must all be true to
return a TRUE result.

Hot tip

You could use an **OR**
function for the first
two countries here, since
the **OR** function returns
TRUE if _either_ of the
comparison expressions
returns TRUE.

Lookup/Reference Functions

If you have a number of items to check against, set up a list. Here is an example using country codes:

1 This worksheet has a vertical list of country names (in alphabetic order) with their dialing codes, stored in a table named "IDC" (International Dialing Codes)

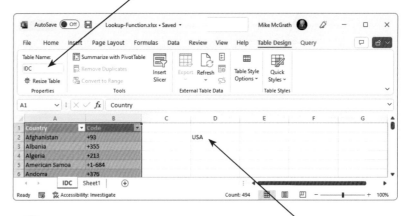

2 To find specific country codes you could type country names in column **D**. For example, type "USA" in **D2**

3 Now, you can use the **VLOOKUP** (vertical lookup) function in column **E** – this requires a value to seek, lookup range, column number for the result, and whether to seek an exact match (**FALSE**) or an approximate match (**TRUE**). So, type **=VLOOKUP($D2, IDC, 2, FALSE)** in **E2**

4 Add more countries in column **D** then copy the formula downward to look up the codes for those countries

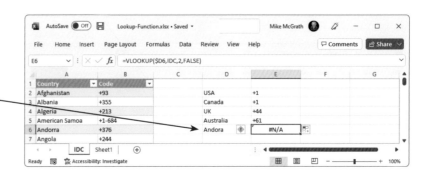

Hot tip

You can have up to 64 levels of nesting, but long **IF** formulas can be awkward to type in. A better alternative may be a **lookup** function.

Don't forget

A mistype of "Andorra" results as **#N/A** here as no exact match is found. Change **FALSE** to **TRUE** in the formula to see an approximate match.

To reverse the process and replace a number with a text value, you could use the **CHOOSE** function. For example:

1 To convert the value of cell **B2** into a rank, enter in **B3** **=CHOOSE(B2,"First","Second","Third","Fourth","Fifth")** – then copy the formula across to Rank cells **C3** to **F3**

Hot tip

The contents of **B2** are used as an index, to select from the list of five values provided. A maximum of 254 values could be used.

2 To apply a suffix to the position value, enter in **B4** the formula **=B2&CHOOSE(B2,"st","nd","rd","th","th")** – then copy the formula across to Standing cells **C4** to **F4**

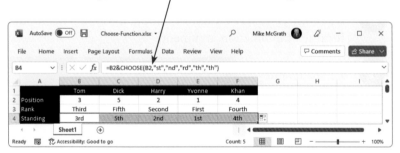

Hot tip

Here, the suffix chosen from the list is appended to the index number.

3 You could store the values in a range of cells, but you must list the relevant cells individually in the formula. Use absolute cell references for the values so that you can copy the formula without having to adjust the references

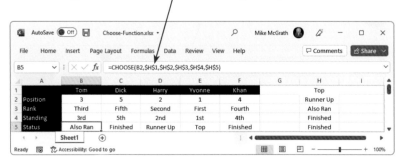

Beware

Index values outside the range provided (in these examples, 1-5) will cause a **#VALUE!** error.

Financial Functions

Excel includes specialized functions for dealing with investments, securities, loans, and other financial transactions. For example, to calculate the monthly payments required for a mortgage, you can use the **PMT** function.

To illustrate this, assume a purchase price of $250,000, interest at 6% per annum, and a 30-year repayment period:

1 Enter the initial information into a worksheet, then, for the payment, begin typing the function **=PMT(**

When you enter a function name, its purpose is displayed. Open its parentheses, and its argument list is displayed.

The amount is shown as a negative number, because it is a payment.

As you select each argument box in the "Function Arguments" dialog, the requirements are described, and you can use the **Collapse** and **Expand** arrow buttons to select values from the worksheet.

2 Click the *fx* **Insert Function** button, to display the input form for the function arguments

3 For **Rate**, put the interest rate per payment period **B2/D2** (6%/12). For **Nper** (number of payments) put **C2*D2** (30*12), and for **Pv** (present value) put **A2** ($250,000)

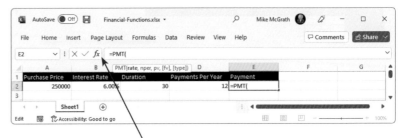

4 Click **OK** to see the payment per month on the worksheet

Perhaps you might like to know what would happen if you paid the mortgage off over a shorter period:

1 Select the existing values and calculation and drag down using the **Fill Handle** (to replicate into three more rows), then change the duration to 25, 20, and 15 years on successive rows – to see revised monthly payments

You could type a new value into the Duration cell and see the new payment. However, copying the rows makes it easier to compare the different options.

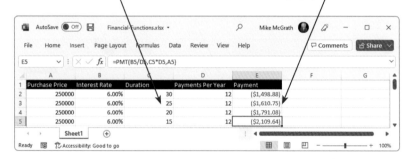

2 Add a column for total interest paid, then enter the cumulative interest payment function **=CUMIPMT(** and click the *fx* **Insert Function** button once more

3 Repeat the values for **Rate**, **Nper**, and **Pv** as for the **PMT** function (opposite), then scroll down the input boxes and enter **Start** at 1, **End** at **C2*D2** and **Type** as 0

Hot tip

You can calculate the interest over any part of the loan, but putting the first and last payments gives the total interest over the whole period of the loan.

4 Copy the formula down, to see the cumulative interest for all the mortgage repayment durations

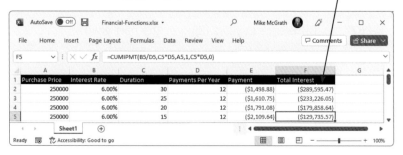

Date & Time Functions

Date and time values (see page 59) are stored as numbers, which are a count of the days since the starting point (usually January 1st, 1900). However, the numeric value can be displayed in various date or time formats as determined by the specified cell format.

1 The whole-number portion of the value converts into month, day, and year (with account taken for leap years), so 46016 represents December 25, 2025

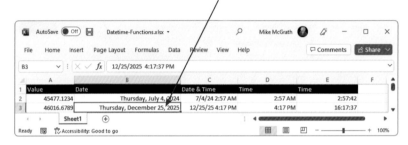

2 The decimal portion of the value indicates the time of day, so .1234 is 2:57 AM, and .6789 is 4:17 PM (16:17)

Hot tip

Excel also supports the 1904 date system – the default for Apple Mac computers, where a date value of 1 is taken as January 2nd, 1904.

Date and Time Calculations

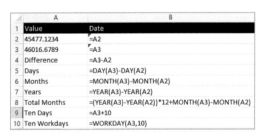

	A	B
1	Value	Date
2	45477.1234	=A2
3	46016.6789	=A3
4	Difference	=A3-A2
5	Days	=DAY(A3)-DAY(A2)
6	Months	=MONTH(A3)-MONTH(A2)
7	Years	=YEAR(A3)-YEAR(A2)
8	Total Months	=(YEAR(A3)-YEAR(A2))*12+MONTH(A3)-MONTH(A2)
9	Ten Days	=A3+10
10	Ten Workdays	=WORKDAY(A3,10)

	A	B
1	Value	Date
2	45477.1234	Thursday, July 4, 2024
3	46016.6789	Thursday, December 25, 2025
4	Difference	540
5	Days	21
6	Months	5
7	Years	1
8	Total Months	17
9	Ten Days	Sunday, January 4, 2026
10	Ten Workdays	Thursday, January 8, 2026

Beware

You can use date and time values in formulas, but, because of the calendar effects, the results may not always be what you'd expect.

B4	Difference in days
B5	Subtracts calendar day numbers (may be minus)
B6	Subtracts calendar months (may be minus)
B7	Difference in years (ignores the part year)
B8	12 months for every year +/- the difference in months
B9	Adding 10 calendar days to A3 gives January 4, 2026
B10	Adding 10 work days (to allow for weekends and holidays) gives the later date January 8, 2026

There's a **DATEDIF** worksheet function that's not listed in the **Date & Time** category (though it is described in Excel **Help**):

=DATEDIF(StartDate, EndDate, Interval)

The **Interval** code controls the result that the function produces:

Interval value	Calculates the number between the dates of
"y"	Whole years
"m"	Whole months
"d"	Days in total
"ym"	Whole months, ignoring the years
"yd"	Days, ignoring the years
"md"	Days, ignoring the months and years

Hot tip

Excel's Visual Basic for Applications (VBA) has a similar function called **DateDiff**, but without the **"ym"**, **"yd"**, and **"md"** interval parameters. Check out Excel VBA in easy steps for more help with this (**www.ineasysteps.com**).

When entering the **Interval** code into **DATEDIF** as a constant, you enclose it in quotes. However, if your **Interval** code is stored in a worksheet cell, it should not be enclosed in quotes in the cell.

1 Use the **DATEDIF** function with each of these codes in turn, to calculate the difference between the dates that are stored in cells **B2** and **B3**

=DATEDIF($B$2,$B$3,"Y")	
G	**H**
	DateDif
Y	1
M	17
D	539
YM	5
YD	174
MD	21

2 This function is useful when calculating someone's exact age in years, months, and days. For example, **DATEDIF** applied to a date of birth and a more current date produces this age:

Hot tip

DATEDIF is applied three times, to obtain the years, months, and days, and the results are joined together into a single statement by the & concatenate operator.

95

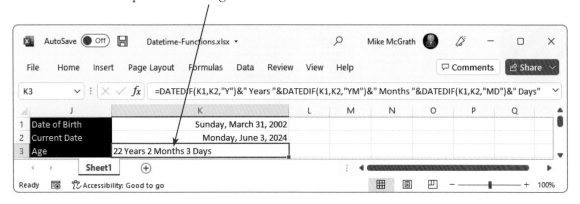

Text Functions

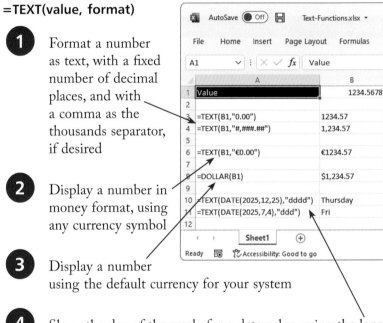

Values can be presented in many different ways, even though they remain stored as numbers. Sometimes, however, you actually want to convert the values into text (enclosed in quotes), perhaps to include them in a specific format in a report or in a message. To do this you would use the **TEXT** function. Its syntax is:

=TEXT(value, format)

1 Format a number as text, with a fixed number of decimal places, and with a comma as the thousands separator, if desired

2 Display a number in money format, using any currency symbol

3 Display a number using the default currency for your system

4 Show the day of the week, for a date value, using the long or short form of the day name

5 For examples of number formats, choose the **Custom** category in the "Format Cells" dialog, and scroll the list

The **DOLLAR** function will display the value in the default currency format for your system; for example, using the Pound Sterling symbol (£) for UK systems.

You can use any of the number formats shown in the **Format Cells** dialog (see page 58), other than **General** format.

There are several functions provided to help you manipulate a piece of text to make it more suitable for presentation:

1 Remove all extraneous blanks, leaving a single space between words

2 Convert all the characters in the text into LOWER case format

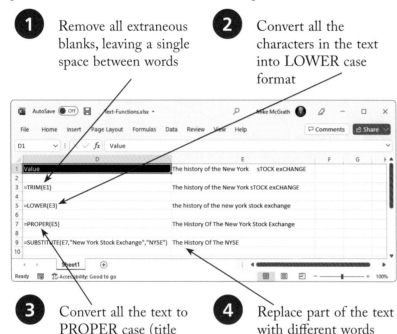

3 Convert all the text to PROPER case (title case)

4 Replace part of the text with different words

Excel does not have an explicit word count function, but the text functions can be used in combination, to find the number of words that are in a cell.

The **TRIM** function removes multiple spaces from the text, then the first **LEN** function counts all the characters, including spaces. The **SUBSTITUTE** function removes all spaces from the text, then the second **LEN** function counts the remaining characters. The difference between the two lengths is the number of spaces between words. Add 1 to find the number of words in the cell.

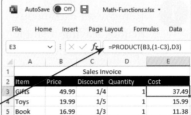

Math & Trig Functions

These functions allow you to carry out calculations using cell contents, computed values, and constants. For example:

1 The **PRODUCT** function multiplies price (B) times quantity (D), then deducts discount (C) to get item cost (E)

2 Copy the formula to calculate the costs for the other items

3 The total net cost is the sum of the costs for all the individual items

You may sometimes want to make calculations without showing all of the intermediate values. For example:

1 Total gross cost before discount is the sum of the products of the item prices and item quantities (**B3*D3 + B4*D4** etc.). This can be calculated with the **SUMPRODUCT** function, which multiplies the sets of cells and totals the results

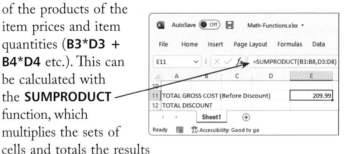

2 Total discount is simply total gross cost minus total net cost. This avoids problems with rounding errors, which can occur even with straightforward functions such as **SUM**

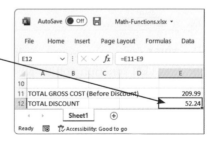

To illustrate the type of problem that can arise, imagine placing an order for goods where there's a special gift offered for spending $140 or more.

1 A quick check seems to indicate that the total is just over the amount required

2 But the total that Excel calculates appears to be just under that amount

	A	B	C	D	E	F
			Sales Invoice			
1						
2	Item	Price	Discount	Quantity	Cost	
3	Gifts	49.99	1/3	1	33.33	
4	Toys	19.99	1/3	1	13.33	
5	Book	16.99	1/3	1	11.33	
6	Pad	1.39	1/3	10	9.27	
7	Flash	13.99	1/3	7	65.29	
8	Gizmo	11.19	1/3	1	7.46	
9	TOTAL NET COST				139.99	?140.01
10		Spend $140 to get that Special Gift!				
11	TOTAL GROSS COST (Before Discount)				209.99	
12	TOTAL DISCOUNT				70.00	

Cell reference: E9 = `=SUM(E3:E8)`

Excel hasn't got its sums wrong – the stored numbers that it totals aren't quite the same as those on display.

33.3266683
13.3266673
11.3266672
9.2666671
65.2866699
7.4600004
139.9933403

3 Change the cell format to show more decimal places, and you'll see that the stored values are slightly lower than those initially shown

4 Click cell **E3**, and add the **ROUND** function – to round the item cost to two places

Cell reference: E3 = `=ROUND(PRODUCT(B3,(1-C3),D3),2)`

	A	B	C	D	E	F
1			Sales Invoice			
2	Item	Price	Discount	Quantity	Cost	
3	Gifts	49.99	1/3	1	33.33	
4	Toys	19.99	1/3	1	13.33	
5	Book	16.99	1/3	1	11.33	
6	Pad	1.39	1/3	10	9.27	
7	Flash	13.99	1/3	7	65.29	
8	Gizmo	11.19	1/3	1	7.46	
9	TOTAL NET COST				140.01	
10		Spend $140 to get that Special Gift!				
11	TOTAL GROSS COST (Before Discount)				209.99	
12	TOTAL DISCOUNT				69.98	

5 Copy the new formula into cells **E4:E8** to see the expected amount

The **ROUND** function rounds up or down. So, 1.234 becomes 1.23, but 1.236 becomes 1.24 (rounded to two decimal places). You can specify a negative number of places to round the values to the nearest multiple of 10 (-1 places) or of 100 (-2 places), and so on.

33.3300000
13.3300000
11.3300000
9.2700000
65.2900000
7.4600000
140.0100000

Random Numbers

It is sometimes useful to produce sets of random numbers. This could be for sample data, when creating or testing worksheets. Another use might be to select a variety of tracks from your music library to generate a playlist.

1 Click **A1** and enter the function **=RAND( )**, to generate a random number between 0 and 1, then copy **A1** down through **A2:A5** and see a different number shown in each cell

Hot tip

RAND generates a number from 0 to 1. **=RAND()*99+101** would give numbers between 101 and 200. Unlike those produced by the **RANDBETWEEN** function, these aren't whole numbers.

2 Click **B1** and enter the function **=RANDBETWEEN(1,10)** then copy **B1** down through **B2:B5** to generate whole numbers less than or equal to 10

3 Click **C1** and enter the function **=RANDBETWEEN(-99,99)** then copy **C1** down through **C2:C5** to generate numbers for each cell between -99 and +99

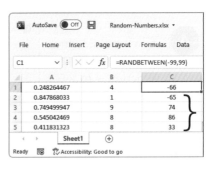

Hot tip

To generate a random number that doesn't change each time the worksheet is recalculated, type **=RAND()** on the Formula bar, and then press **F9**. The generated number is placed into the cell as a literal value.

4 Select the **Formulas** tab, click **Calculate Now** in the [**Calculation**] group, and all the numbers will be regenerated

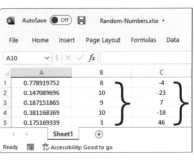

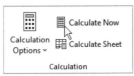

Statistical Functions

There's a large number of statistical functions, but the most likely one to be used is the **AVERAGE** function.

1 Create a block **A1:E5** of random numbers between 101 and 200 to use as data for the functions

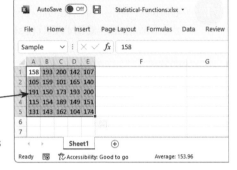

2 Define "Sample" as the name for the range **$A$1:$E$5**

3 Select and copy **A1:E5**, then select **Home**, [**Clipboard**] then click the arrow on the **Paste** command. Now, select **Paste Values** to replace the formula with the literal value in each cell

4 The arithmetic mean of the sample is **=AVERAGE(Sample)** and the number in the middle of the sample is **=MEDIAN(Sample)**

5 The most frequently-occurring value is **=MODE(Sample)** and the number of values is **=COUNT(Sample)**

6 The number of values in the sample that are greater than or equal to 150 is **=COUNTIF(Sample,">=150")**

7 The maximum value in the sample is **=MAX(Sample)** and the minimum value in the sample is **=MIN(Sample)**

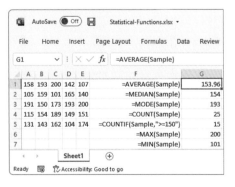

Hot tip

Using **Copy**, **Paste**, then **Paste Values** to replace the formulas with their values means that the set of random numbers generated won't later be affected by recalculation of the worksheet.

Don't forget

There are a number of different ways to interpret the term "average". Make sure that you use the function that's appropriate for your requirements.

Engineering Functions

There are some rather esoteric functions in the **Engineering** category, but some are quite generally applicable. For example:

1 Convert from one measurement system to another, using the function **=CONVERT(value, from_unit, to_unit)**

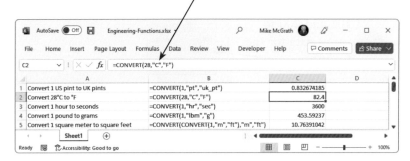

This function deals with units of weight and mass, distance, time, pressure, force, energy, power, magnetism, temperature, and liquids. There are functions to convert between any two pairs of number systems, including binary, decimal, hexadecimal, and octal.

2 Convert decimal values to their binary, octal, and hexadecimal equivalents

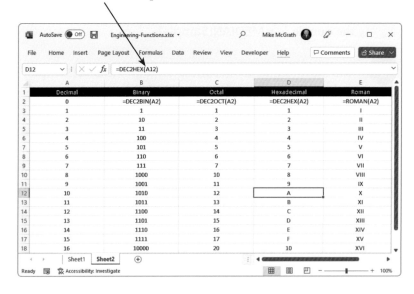

=ROMAN(1499,0)	MCDXCIX
=ROMAN(1499,1)	MLDVLIV
=ROMAN(1499,2)	MXDIX
=ROMAN(1499,3)	MVDIV
=ROMAN(1499,4)	MID

There's a **ROMAN** function, which converts Arabic numerals to Roman numerals, but it comes from the **Math & Trig** category, which also has an **ARABIC** function for the reverse process.

Excel Add-ins

There are **Add-ins** included with Excel, but they must be loaded before they can be used:

1 Click the **File** tab,, then click the **Options** button

2 Click the **Add-ins** category and, in the **Manage** box, select **Excel Add-ins**, then click **Go...**

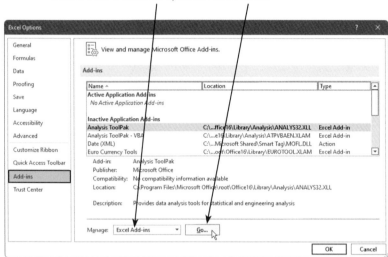

Hot tip

If you are still looking for the functions you need, you may find them in an **Excel Add-in**, such as the **Analysis ToolPak** or the **Solver Add-in**.

3 To load an Excel **Add-in**, select the associated check box, then click **OK**

4 You may be prompted to install some of the Add-in programs that you select

Don't forget

To unload an Excel **Add-in**, clear the associated check box, then click **OK**. This does not delete the **Add-in** from your computer.

5 The new functions that have been added can be found on the **Formulas** tab in the [**Solutions**] group, or on the **Data** tab in the [**Analyze**] group

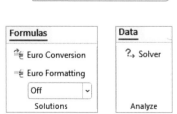

Evaluate Formula

If you are not sure exactly how a formula works, especially when there are nested functions, use the **Evaluate** command to run the formula one step at a time. To use this:

1 Select the cell with the formula you wish to investigate, then choose the **Formulas** tab, in the [**Formula Auditing**] group, and select the **Evaluate Formula** command

This is the formula for rounding item costs, as shown in Step 4 on page 99.

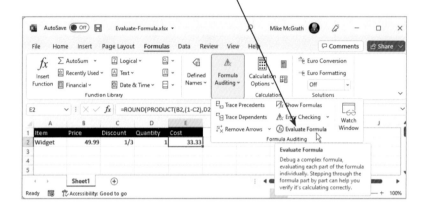

104

Don't forget

Press the **Step In** button to check details like the value of a constant, or to see the expansion of range or table names. Press the **Step Out** button to carry on with the evaluation. Press the **Close** button when you reach the end, or see that the **Evaluate** button has changed to **Restart** so that you can run through the steps again.

2 Press **Evaluate** repeatedly, to run the calculation forward, one step at a time

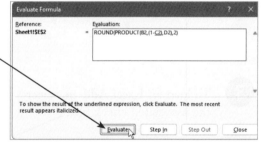

3 See the expressions in the formula calculated in turn and the intermediate values get displayed at each step

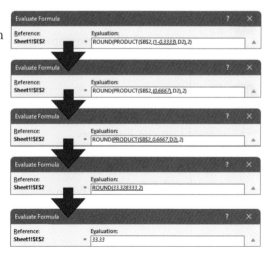

7 Control Excel

Keep control of your worksheets, audit the formulas, and check for errors. Make backup copies, and use the automatic save and recover capabilities. You can also control Excel through startup switches, shortcuts, Key Tips for the Ribbon commands, and the Quick Access and Mini Toolbars.

Audit Formulas

1 Click the **Formulas** tab, to see the [**Formula Auditing**] group

2 If the commands are grayed, click the **File** tab, select the **Options** item, then click **Advanced**

Hot tip

When you are reviewing a worksheet and the formulas it contains, use the tools in the [**Formula Auditing**] group.

3 Make sure that the **All** option is selected in the **Display options for this workbook** section

4 Select a cell, and click the **Trace Precedents** icon in the [**Formula Auditing**] group

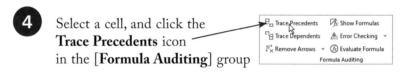

Don't forget

Precedents are those cells that are referred to by the formula in the selected cell.

5 You will see a warning message if the cell, such as **B3**, has no formula

6 With a cell that does contain a formula, such as **E9**, the line arrow and box show the cells that are directly referred to by that formula

Beware

The cell you select must contain a formula for the **Trace Precedents** button to operate.

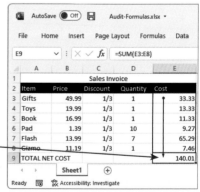

7 Click **Trace Precedents**, to see the next level of cells (if the first level of precedent cells refer to more cells)

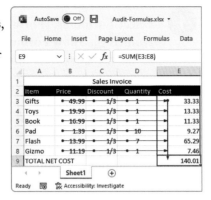

8 Now, click the **Trace Dependents** icon to show the cells that rely on the value in the selected cell

9 Click the **Remove Arrows** icon, in the [**Formula Auditing**] group

Don't forget

Dependents are those cells that contain formulas that refer to the selected cell.

107

You can analyze the role of cells that contain only literal values:

1 Click a cell (e.g. **B2**) that contains no formula, then click **Trace Dependents**

2 If there are no cell references, you will again receive a warning message

3 Select **B3**, and click **Trace Dependents** three times to see the references to that cell

Hot tip

If you press **Trace Dependents** multiple times you can see the direct and the indirect references to the value in the selected cell.

Protect Formulas

1 Select **Formulas**, [**Formula Auditing**], **Show Formulas** to see the worksheet formulas

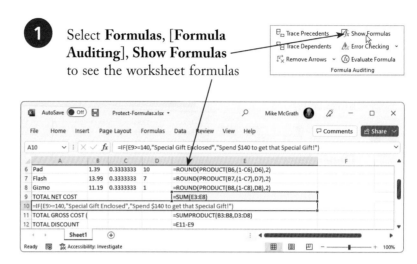

2 To hide a formula, select the cell, then click the **Home** tab, in the [**Cells**] group, **Format**, and **Format Cells...**

3 In the "Format Cells" dialog, click the **Protection** tab, then check the box labeled **Hidden** and click **OK**

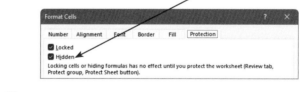

4 Select the **Home** tab, in the [**Cells**] group, **Format**, and **Protect Sheet...** then click **OK** on the "Protect Sheet" dialog to activate protection and hide the formula

Check for Errors

Excel applies rules to check for potential errors in formulas:

1 Click the **File** tab, select **Options**, then click **Formulas**

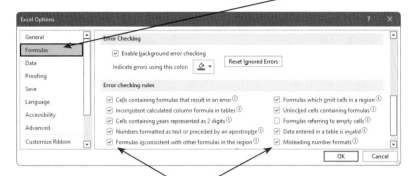

Hot tip

Some errors will just be warnings, and some may be due to information not yet recorded.

2 Select or clear the check boxes to change the errors that Excel will detect

3 Select **Formulas**, [**Formula Auditing**], and click the arrow beside the **Error Checking** item

4 Click **Error Checking...** on the drop-down menu to review any errors, and make corrections on the **Formula bar**

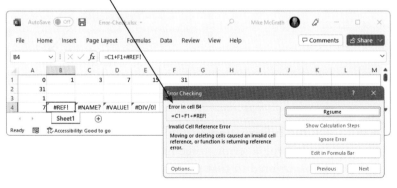

Beware

If the worksheet has previously been checked, any **Ignored** errors will not appear until you press the **Reset Ignored Errors** button, in **File**, **Options**, **Formulas**.

5 Click the **Next** button, to review each remaining error in turn

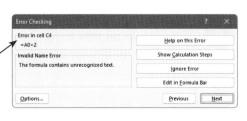

...cont'd

You can also review individual errors on the worksheet:

1 Click an error, then select **Formulas**, [**Formula Auditing**], **Error Checking**, **Trace Error** from the drop-down menu

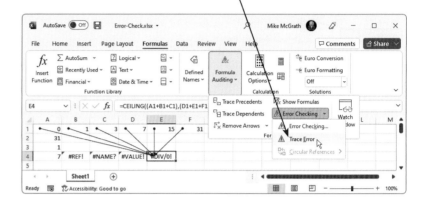

2 You can select **Circular References** to see the cells that refer to their own contents, directly or indirectly

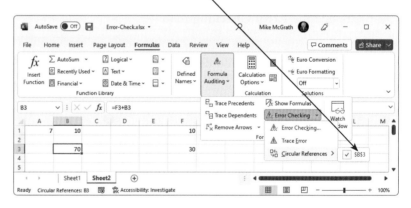

Hot tip

The **Error Checking** options become very useful when you have large worksheets, where errors and warnings are off screen and out of view.

3 Click the **Information** button on an individual error to see more options, tailored to that particular type of error

4 Click **Help on this Error** for assistance on how to fix this error

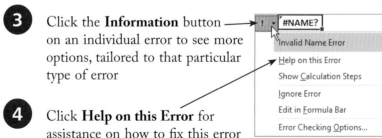

Backup

1 To make a copy of your workbook, click the **File** tab and select **Open** (or press the **Ctrl** + **O** shortcut keys)

2 Right-click the file for the workbook, then select **Copy** from the context menu

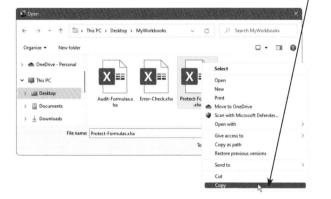

3 Switch to the backup folder, then right-click an empty area and select **Paste** from the context menu

4 The file is copied to the folder and you are warned if there's already a copy in the backup folder

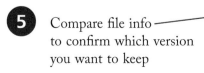

5 Compare file info to confirm which version you want to keep

When you are working on a large worksheet it is often helpful to make a copy before you apply significant changes so that you can undo them, if necessary.

You can keep extra copies of your workbooks in your OneDrive (see pages 180-181).

If there's already a copy, Windows compares the two versions and lets you choose to replace the file, or skip copying the workbook.

AutoSave and AutoRecover

To review and adjust the **AutoRecover** and **AutoSave** settings:

1 Click the **File** tab, then click **Options** and select **Save**

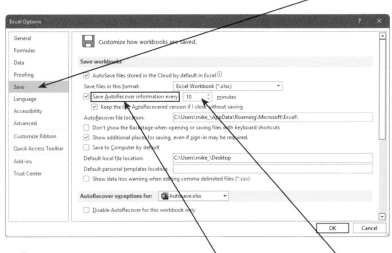

Hot tip

Excel will automatically save your worksheet periodically, and can recover the file if your system shuts down in the middle of an update.

2 Check the **Save AutoRecover information** box, review the frequency, then click **OK** to save any changes

3 Restart your system without saving the current changes, then open Excel to be given the opportunity to recover your changes – as recorded up to the last **AutoSave**

Hot tip

The **Document Recovery** task pane displays up to three versions of your file, with the most recent at the top.

4 Select a recovered entry, click the drop-down arrow and choose **Save As...** to choose that version – or select the original version to discard changes

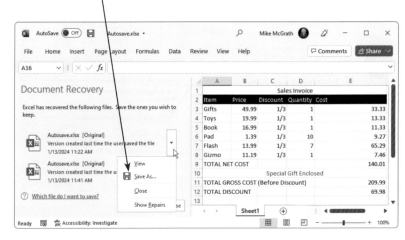

Don't forget

Excel will keep the last **AutoSave** version, even when you deliberately close without saving, so you can still recover your latest changes.

Startup Switches

When you start Excel in the usual way, the Excel splash screen is displayed, and the Excel Start screen then opens where you can select a new blank workbook, a recent workbook, or a template.

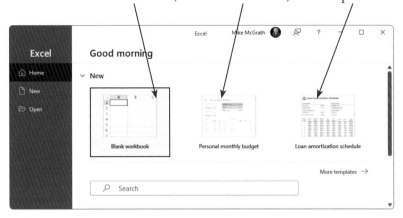

You can create a shortcut to Excel, with your required parameters, and place this on the desktop or the taskbar – described on page 114.

1 To start Excel without the splash screen or the selection panel, press the **Windows key** + **R**, type in **excel.exe /e** then click **OK**

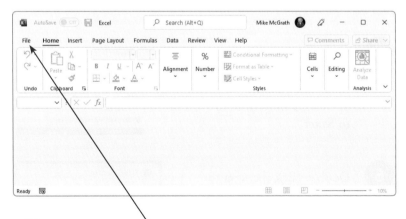

Start Excel in safe mode by typing **excel.exe / safe**. This can be useful if you are having problems opening a particular workbook.

2 Select the **File** tab to create a new workbook or to open an existing workbook

You can specify a workbook path and name and have Excel start with that workbook. For example, you might type the **excel.exe /e "C:\Data\mybudget.xlsx"** command into the **Run** box.

Create a Shortcut

To create a shortcut to load Excel using the startup switches discussed on page 113:

1 Locate the **Excel.exe** file on your hard drive, typically at **C:\Program Files\Microsoft Office\root\Office16\Excel.exe**

2 Right-click the Desktop, then select **New, Shortcut**

3 Browse to the **Excel.exe** file location and select it, then add the required switch (e.g. **/e** or **/safe**) outside the quote marks

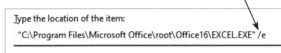

If necessary, use Windows Search to locate the **Excel.exe** program, and then note the location.

Hot tip

4 Name the new shortcut, then click **Finish** to create a shortcut icon on the Desktop

> Type a name for this shortcut:
>
> Excel QuickStart

Don't forget

Make sure that you enter a space between the final quote mark and the command-line switch.

5 Right-click the shortcut icon on the Desktop, then select **Show more options, Pin to taskbar** (or **Pin to Start**)

6 Double-click the icon to launch the program using the startup switches

7 To create a shortcut for a specific workbook, right-click its file icon then choose **Show more options, Send to, Desktop (create shortcut)**

Ribbon Key Tips

Although the Ribbon is designed for mouse and touch selection, it is still possible to carry out any task available on the Ribbon without moving your hands from the keyboard:

① Press **Ctrl**, **Home** to select the first worksheet cell, then press and release **Alt** (or press **F10**) to show **Key Tips**

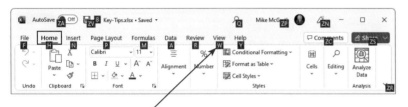

② Press the letter for the command tab that you want to display – for example, press **W** for **View**

③ Press the letter(s) for the commands or group that you want to use – for example, press **ZS** for **Show/Hide**, then press **VF** to hide the **Formula bar**

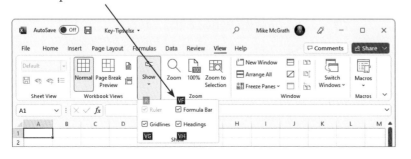

Hot tip

Press and release the **Alt** key again (or press **F10**) to hide **Key Tips**.

Don't forget

Key Tips change when you select a tab, and further **Key Tips** display when you select specific commands.

Hot tip

It doesn't matter if **Alt** is pressed or not – the shortcut keys in the **Key Tips** will still operate. You can also use uppercase or lowercase.

Using Key Tips

1 To go to a specific cell (**C7**, for example), first press **Alt** to show the **Key Tips**

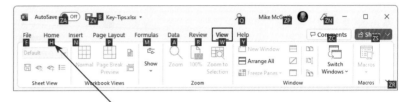

2 Next, press **H** to switch to the **Home** tab

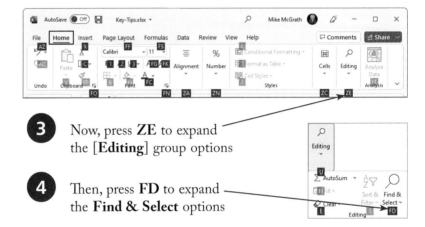

3 Now, press **ZE** to expand the [**Editing**] group options

4 Then, press **FD** to expand the **Find & Select** options

5 Press **G** to launch the "Go To" dialog

6 Enter the cell address (**C7**, in this case) then press **Enter** to see **C7** now become the active cell

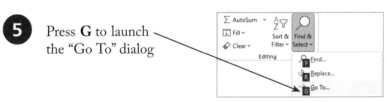

7 With **C7** selected, to insert **AutoSum** press **Alt**, then **H** to show **Key Tips** on the **Home** tab

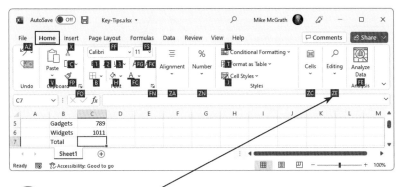

You can insert the **AutoSum** function into the active cell using keystrokes only.

8 Next, press **ZE** to expand the [**Editing**] group options

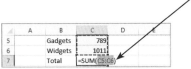

9 Now, press **U** to expand the **AutoSum** options

ZE expands the [**Editing**] group, but you can bypass this and go straight to **U** (**AutoSum**) if you don't need the visual prompt.

10 Then, press **S** to select the **Sum** function and see the formula get added to **C7**

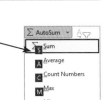

11 Finally, press **Enter** to see the result appear in cell **C7**

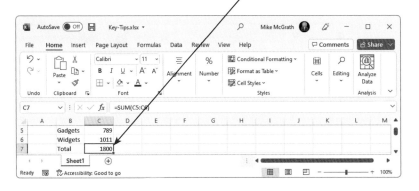

For tasks that you perform often, the **Key Tips** option can become the quickest way to operate, as you become familiar with the keystrokes needed.

117

Collapse the Ribbon

1 Right-click the Ribbon's **Tab Bar**, then select **Collapse the Ribbon** (or click the **Ribbon Display Options** button and select **Show tabs only**) to collapse the Ribbon

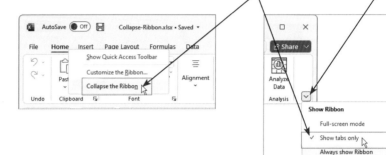

Hot tip

To expand a collapsed Ribbon, double-click the current tab, or press keys **Ctrl** + **F1**, or select **Always Show Ribbon** from the **Ribbon Display Options** menu.

2 With the Ribbon collapsed, click any tab to display the Ribbon temporarily to select commands from that tab

3 The **Alt** key and the **Key Tips** still operate, even when you have collapsed the Ribbon

Hot tip

When you launch Excel the Ribbon will be in the same state as it was when Excel last closed.

Quick Access Toolbar

The **Quick Access Toolbar** can contain commands that are independent of the particular command tab being displayed. Initially, there may be a single command (**Quick Print**) plus a drop-down button allowing you to **Customize Quick Access Toolbar**. By default, the **Quick Access Toolbar** is located below the Ribbon, but you can move it onto the Excel **Title bar**.

1 Click the Ribbon's **Ribbon Display Options** button and select **Show Quick Access Toolbar**

2 Click the drop-down button on the **Quick Access Toolbar** and select **Show Above the Ribbon** from the drop-down menu

3 To add a command, select **More Commands...** from the drop-down menu

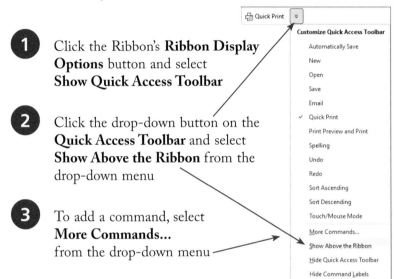

When you select a menu entry, the instruction gets modified to show the reverse process.

You can also right-click any command on the Ribbon, then select **Add to Quick Access Toolbar** from the menu.

4 Choose a category, select a command, click **Add**, then click **OK** to place that command on the **Quick Access Toolbar** – for example, **AutoFit Column Width**

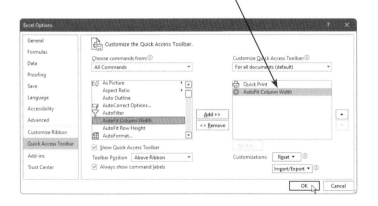

To restore the position, click the drop-down button on the **Quick Access Toolbar** and select **Show Below the Ribbon**.

Mini Toolbar

The **Mini Toolbar** appears when you select text, or when editing the contents of a cell (and also when working with charts and text boxes). It offers quick access to the tools you need for text editing, such as font, size, style, alignment, color, and bullets. To see the **Mini Toolbar**:

1 Choose a cell containing text content

2 Select (highlight) part or all of the text and see the **Mini Toolbar** appear above the cell

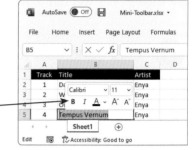

3 Use the **Mini Toolbar** to modify the selected text's font style, color and/or size

4 Move the mouse pointer away from the toolbar, and see the **Mini Toolbar** disappear

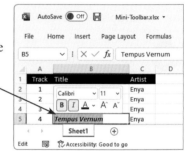

The **Mini Toolbar** feature was created as an extension of the context right-click menu, and it may appear whenever that menu appears.

5 Select a cell containing text, then right-click the cell without selecting text to see the **Mini Toolbar** appear above the context menu

Don't forget

The **Mini Toolbar** that appears by right-clicking in a cell provides more options than those when text has been selected.

Print Worksheets

To preview printing for multiple worksheets:

1 Open the workbook, then click the tab for the first sheet

2 To select adjacent sheets, hold down the **Shift** key, then click the tab for the last sheet in the group

3 To add other non-adjacent sheets, hold down the **Ctrl** key, then click the tabs for all other required sheets

Beware

If you change any cell while multiple sheets are selected, the change is automatically applied to all selected sheets.

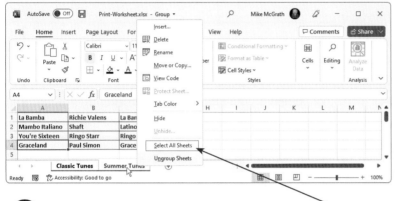

4 To select all the sheets, right-click any tab, then click **Select All Sheets**

5 Click the **File** tab and select **Print** (or press **Ctrl** + **F2**), to see the **Printer** details and the various settings

6 If you prefer to use **Key Tips**, press **Alt** + **F** – **P** – **V**

The **Preview** pane shows previews of print pages for sheets that you selected.

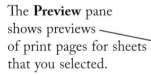

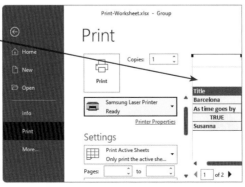

Don't forget

When multiple sheets are selected, the term **[Group]** appears on the Excel Title bar.

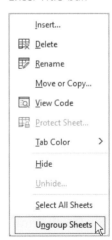

To cancel the selection, click any unselected tab, or right-click any tab and click **Ungroup Sheets**.

...cont'd

Review the print preview pages before sending to the printer:

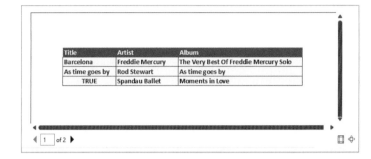

Title	Artist	Album
Barcelona	Freddie Mercury	The Very Best Of Freddie Mercury Solo
As time goes by	Rod Stewart	As time goes by
TRUE	Spandau Ballet	Moments in Love

◀ 1 of 2 ▶

Title	Artist	Album
La Bamba	Richie Valens	La Bamba
Mambo Italiano	Shaft	Latino Summer
You're Sixteen	Ringo Starr	Ringo
Graceland	Paul Simon	Graceland

◀ 2 of 2 ▶

Hot tip

Click the **Page Setup** link to make detailed changes to the print settings. Click the **Printer Properties** link to control the printer.

122

Don't forget

If the settings are already as you want them, you can use the **Quick Print** button (see page 33) to start the print without previewing.

1 Click the **Next Page** arrow to go forward, or click the **Previous Page** arrow to go back

2 Click the ⊞ **Show Margins** button, to display margins. Click and drag the margins to adjust their positions

3 Click the ⟨⊹⟩ **Zoom to Page** button to switch the preview between close-up and full-page views

4 Click the **Settings** options to adjust items such as paper size, orientation, scaling, and collation `▭ Landscape Orientation ▾`

5 Click the **Printer** button to check the different printer options available `▤ Samsung Laser Printer / Ready ▾`

6 Click the **Print** button to carry out the actual printing of the selected sheets `🖶 Print`

8 Charts

Excel makes it easy to turn your worksheet data into a chart. You can apply formatting, change the type, reselect data, and add effects such as 3-D display. Special chart types allow you to display data for stocks and shares. You can print the completed charts on their own, or as part of a worksheet.

Create a Chart

The following fictitious information about share purchases and prices will be used to illustrate the Excel charting features:

- Total value of shares in a portfolio at start of each year (to chart).
- The individual prices of the shares on those dates (to calculate).
- The total number of shares held (kept constant for simplicity).

To create a chart you can modify and format later, start by entering data on a worksheet. Then, select the data and choose the chart type.

You can select non-adjacent cells or ranges as long as the final selection forms a rectangle. You can also hide rows or columns that you don't need.

If you let Excel choose the data, ensure there is a blank row and column between the data you want to plot and other data on the worksheet.

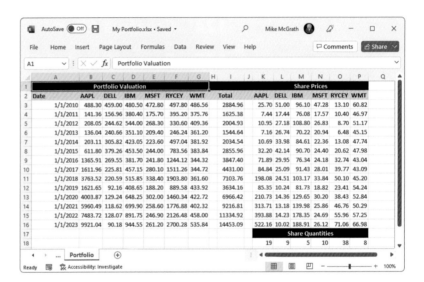

Select Data

Some chart types, such as pie and bubble charts, require a specific data arrangement. For most chart types, however – including line, column, and bar charts – you can use the data as arranged in the rows and columns of the worksheet.

1 Select the cells that contain the data that you want to use for the chart

2 Alternatively, click any cell in a block of data and let Excel select the whole block

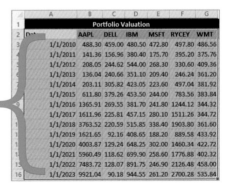

...cont'd

3 Click the **Insert** tab, then select a chart type (for example, select **Column** from the [**Charts**] group)

4 Choose the chart subtype – e.g. **2-D Stacked Column** – to show how each share contributes to the total value

5 The chart is superimposed over the data on the worksheet – see that **Chart Design** and **Format** tabs are now added to the Ribbon

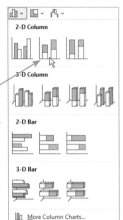

When you move the mouse pointer over any of the chart subtypes, you get a description and an indication of when that chart subtype might prove useful.

Stacked Column

Use this chart type to:
• Compare parts of a whole.
• Show how parts of a whole change over time.

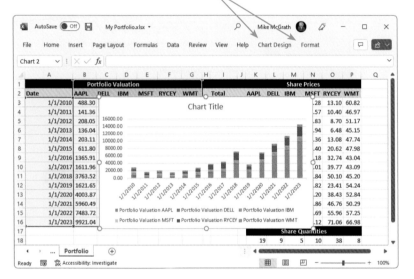

6 Click **Move Chart** in the [**Location**] group on the **Chart Design** tab, to choose where you want the chart to be placed. For example, choose **New sheet** to create a separate chart sheet, and accept the default name of "Chart1"

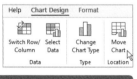

You can also move the chart on the worksheet by clicking on the border and dragging it to another part of the worksheet.

Recommended Chart Type

Excel will recommend chart types for your selected data:

1 Select **Insert**, [**Charts**] group, **Recommended Charts** (or click the corner arrow on the group)

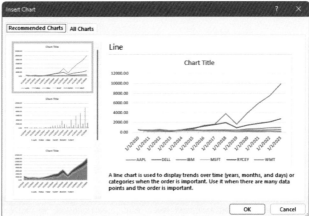

The **Recommended Charts** command lets you pick from a variety of charts that are right for your data.

2 Click the **All Charts** tab to see the range of charts

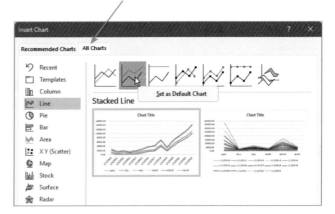

The usual default chart type is a **2-D Clustered Column**, which uses vertical rectangles to compare values across categories.

3 Right-click any chart type and select **Set as Default Chart** from the context menu

The **2-D Stacked Line** chart selected as the new default shows the trend in the contribution, from each of the categories.

4 With a data range selected, press **F11** and the default chart type is displayed on a chart sheet, using the next free name ("Chart2", in this case)

Change Chart Layout

Select **Quick Layout** from **Chart Layouts** on the **Chart Design** tab to quickly try out some predefined chart layouts.

1 Select the **Chart Design** tab and click **Add Chart Element**

2 Select **Chart Title** and choose **Above Chart**

3 Right-click the sample words "Chart Title", then select **Edit Text** to amend the wording, and **Font...** to amend the style

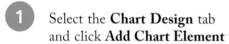

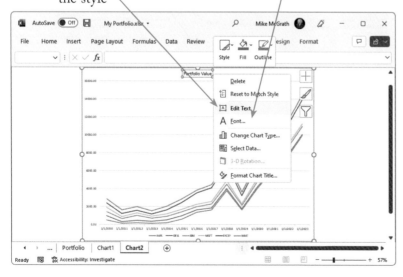

In the same way, you can add **Axis Titles** and adjust the **Gridlines**.

Instead of typing the titles directly, link to a cell on the worksheet. Click in the title, type = on the Formula bar, select the cell with the text, then press **Enter**.

128

Legend and Data Table

1 Select **Chart Design**, [**Chart Layouts**], **Add Chart Element**, **Legend** and choose its position and alignment on the chart – for example, choose **Right**

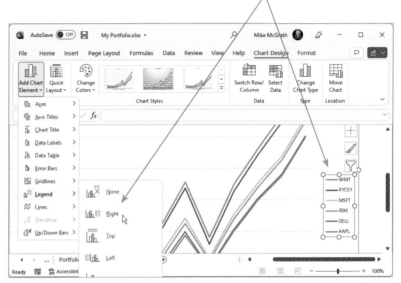

Hot tip

The **Legend** provides the key to the entries on the chart; in this case, the stock symbols for all of the shares.

Hot tip

You can also display data labels to show the data values at each point on the lines.

2 To show the full details, click **Add Chart Element**, **Data Table**, and choose options such as **With Legend Keys**

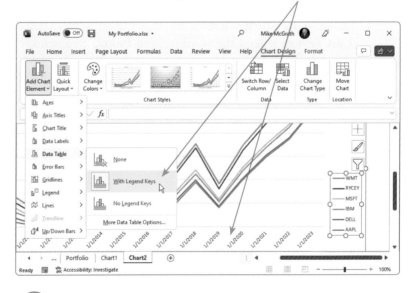

Don't forget

If you show the data for the chart in a table and include **Legend** keys, you can then select **None** to turn off the display of the **Legend**.

3 Again, you can adjust the text size and style for the entries in the **Legend** and the **Data Table**

Change Chart Type

1 Select the **Chart Design** tab, and click **Change Chart Type** from the [**Type**] group

2 In the "Change Chart Type" dialog, select the chart type and subtype – for example, choose chart type **Area** and subtype **Stacked Area**, then click **OK**

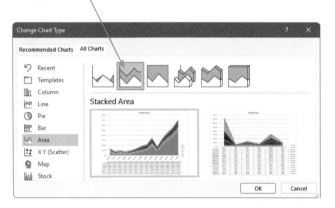

3 The **Chart Design**, [**Chart Styles**] group allows you to change the colors and the overall visual style for your chart

Chart Styles

Hot tip

The **Map** chart type recognizes data such as countries or states, and displays data on an appropriate map.

States	Population
CA	39536653
TX	28304596
FL	20984400
NY	19849399
PA	12805537
IL	12802023
OH	11658609
GA	10429379
NC	10273419

Don't forget

When you change the chart style, you may need to apply other changes such as text font sizes.

Pie Chart

1 Select data labels and one set of data in an adjacent row (or hold down **Ctrl** to select non-adjacent cells)

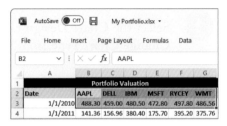

	A	B	C	D	E	F	G
1			Portfolio Valuation				
2	Date	AAPL	DELL	IBM	MSFT	RYCEY	WMT
3	1/1/2010	488.30	459.00	480.50	472.80	497.80	486.56
4	1/1/2011	141.36	156.96	380.40	175.70	395.20	375.76

2 Click the **Insert** tab, select **Pie** from the [**Charts**] group, and choose the chart type – for example, choose the standard **2-D Pie** chart

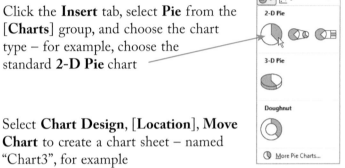

A pie chart compares the contributions of individual items to the total. This is intended for a single set of data such as a year's share values.

3 Select **Chart Design**, [**Location**], **Move Chart** to create a chart sheet – named "Chart3", for example

4 From the **Chart Design** tab, select **Quick Layout** in the [**Chart Layouts**] group

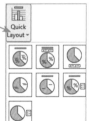

5 Choose one of the predefined layouts from the drop-down selection with the arrangement you prefer

Excel will first load a placeholder for large charts, then load text right away – so you can start editing immediately.

Right-click a data label then choose **Format Data Labels**, then choose what you want to appear on the label. Shown here are **Category** and **Percentage** options.

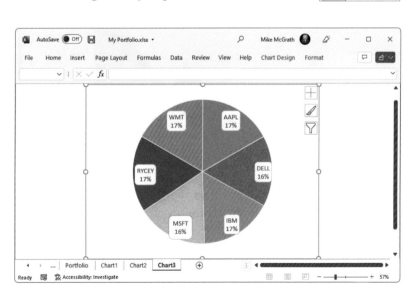

You can change the data series selected for the chart:

1 Select the **Chart Design** tab, then click the
[**Data**], **Select Data** command.
(Here, the selected data range is for 2010)

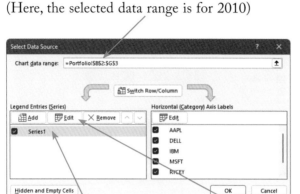

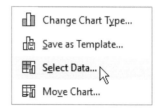

You can also right-click the chart and choose **Select Data...** to modify the data source settings.

2 Click the data series ("Series1"), then click the **Edit** button

3 Edit the chart data range to select a new data range – such as the 2023 values

4 Click **OK** to update the pie chart for the new period

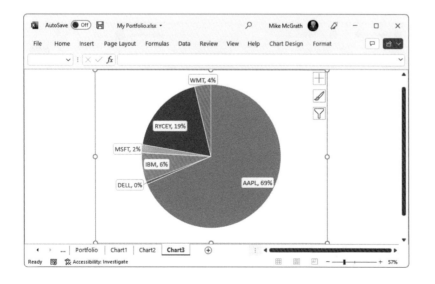

Notice that Excel may decide to put the data label outside the segment if the text won't fit into the space available.

131

3-D Pie Chart

One of the subtypes for the pie chart offers a 3-D view.

1 Select the **Chart Design** tab, and click [**Type**], **Change Chart Type**. Select **Pie**, **3-D Pie**, then click **OK**

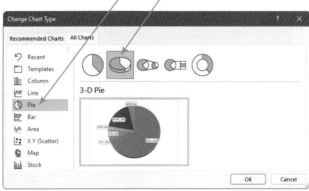

Don't forget

In a 3-D pie chart, it is the chart segments that are displayed in 3-D format, rather than the data itself (hence the grayed Z component).

2 Right-click the chart and select **3-D Rotation**. Set preset rotation values (e.g. **X**: 270°, **Y**: 30°, **Perspective**: 15°), then click **Close**

3 The information is presented in 3-D display form. You can adjust the appearance with **Change Colors** and **Chart Styles**

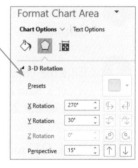

Hot tip

Experiment with the rotation and format options to find the most effective presentation form for your data.

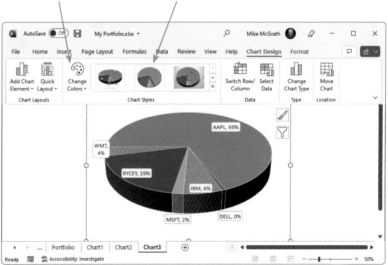

3-D Column Chart

A true 3-D chart has three sets of values to plot, giving three axes. In the example data, these are "Shares", "Values", and "Dates".

1 Select the data, then click **Insert**, **[Charts]**, **Column** and select the **3-D Column** chart type

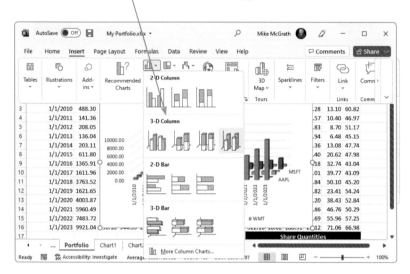

Hot tip

The **3-D Area** chart also presents data using three axes, to give a true 3-D representation.

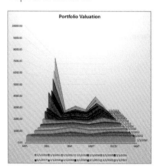

2 Right-click the chart and select **3-D Rotation** to change orientation and perspective if desired

3 Right-click the chart and choose **Move Chart** from the context menu, then select **New sheet** (named "Chart4")

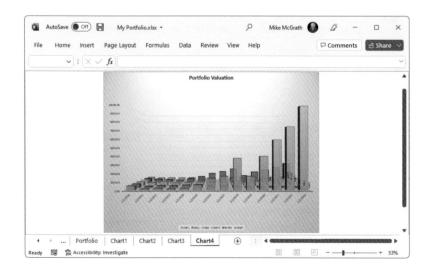

Hot tip

Click **Chart Design**, **Select Data**, and click the **Switch Row/ Column** button to exchange the horizontal and depth axes, to give a different view of the data.

Share Price Data

1 Go to **finance.yahoo.com**, search for a stock symbol (**MSFT**, for example), then click the **Historical Data** link

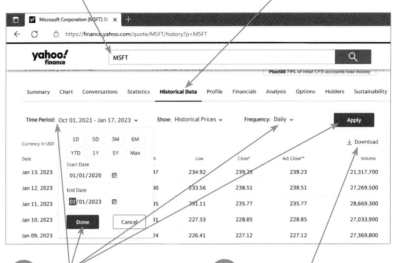

Don't forget

The share prices in a portfolio worksheet could be taken from price history tables downloaded from the Yahoo! Finance website.

Beware

The price history table on **Yahoo! Finance** gives information in reverse date sequence, on a daily, weekly, or monthly basis. Use the **Adjusted Close** (Adj Close) values to ensure comparable prices over time.

2 Specify the **Time Period** and the **Frequency**, then click **Done, Apply**

3 Click **Download** and save the CSV file to your computer

4 Import the data into a spreadsheet (see pages 42-43) as a table named "MSFT"

5 Use a lookup function, as shown below, to find the share price on any valid day within the specified time period

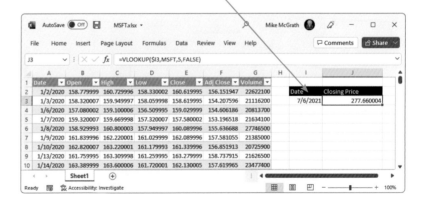

Hot tip

See page 90 for an example of using the **VLOOKUP** function.

Line Chart

The charts, so far, have used just a few dates from the tables. The complete tables, however, provide a continuous view of the data.

1 The Portfolio worksheet contains the adjusted closing price column for each of the shares on each date. Note that for ease of display, the rows for years 2010-2017 have been hidden – so the chart will be for 2018-2023 only

2 Select the data, click **Insert**, [**Charts**], **Insert Line or Area Chart**, then choose a **2-D Line** chart to plot each share

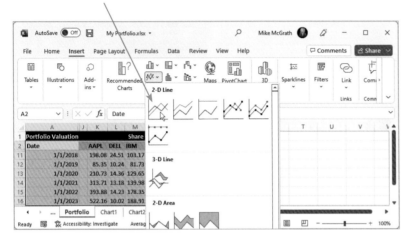

Don't forget

You can move any chart to a separate chart sheet and adjust position and styles for the **Chart Title** and the **Legend**.

135

3 Right-click the chart and choose **Move Chart** from the context menu, then select **New sheet** (named "Chart5")

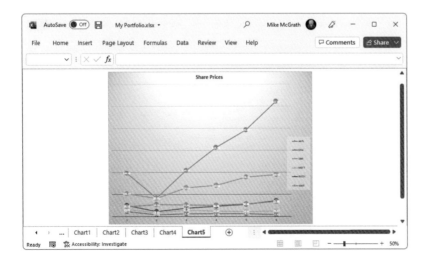

Hot tip

You can choose line, stacked line, or 100% stacked line (with or without markers). There's also a **3-D Line**, but this is just a perspective view, not three axes of data.

Stock Chart

The downloaded share data can also be used for a special type of chart, known as a **Stock** chart.

1 From the shares table, filter the data (e.g. for 2022), then select the columns for **Date**, **Open**, **High**, **Low**, and **Close**

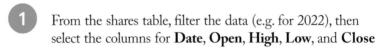

This chart type requires data in a specific layout for the chart subtype; e.g. **High-Low-Close** or **Open-High-Low-Close** (and the date values can be used as data labels).

2 Select **Insert**, **[Charts]**, **Insert Waterfall** etc. Choose **Stock** charts and type as **Open-High-Low-Close**, then click **OK**

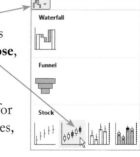

3 The prices are plotted, with lines for high/low, hollow boxes for increases, and solid boxes for decreases

Move the chart to a separate chart sheet, add titles, and format the titles and the **Legend**. Right-click the axis, and select **Format Axis** to change the minimum and maximum, to emphasize price spreads.

Mixed Types

You can have more than one type of chart displayed at the same time, as in the **Volume** subtypes of the **Stock** chart.

1 Cut the **Volume** column, then right-click the **Open** column and choose **Insert Cut Cells** to move the **Volume** column to a position between the **Date** and **Open** columns

You need to rearrange the data downloaded from **Yahoo! Finance** to create volume Stock charts, since volumes must be listed before the various share prices.

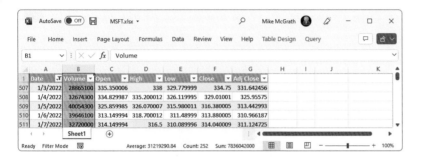

2 Select the headings and the data (for year 2022)

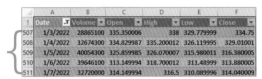

3 Select **Insert**, [**Charts**], **Insert Waterfall** etc. Choose **Stock** charts, select type as **Volume-Open-High-Low-Close**, then click **OK**

137

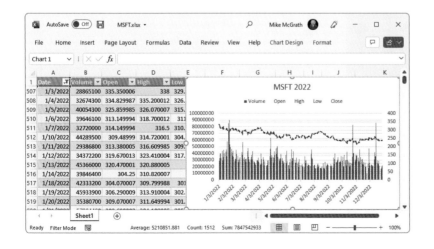

In this example, the two types of chart use the same horizontal values (dates). When necessary, however, Excel will specify a secondary horizontal axis.

Print Charts

When you have an embedded chart in your worksheet, it prints as positioned along with the data when you select **Print** from the **File** tab and click the **Print** button. To print a chart on its own:

1 Select a chart, then select the **File** tab and click **Print**

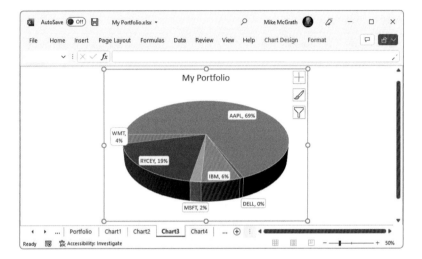

Hot tip

The chart may obscure part of the data. Select **View**, **Page Break Preview** in the **Workbook Views** tab, and drag the chart to reposition it before printing the worksheet.

2 If the worksheet contains data in addition to a chart, an extra **Print Selected Chart** option appears, and other options are grayed out so that only the chart will print

Don't forget

When the chart is in a separate chart sheet, you can print it on its own or as part of the workbook, just as you print a worksheet.

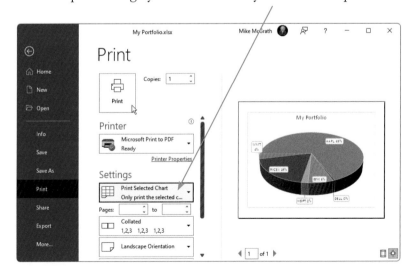

9 Macros in Excel

If there are tasks that you carry out frequently, you can define the actions required, as a macro. You can assign the macro to a key combination or to an icon on the toolbar to make it easy to reuse. However, you must make sure that security is in place to prevent abuse.

Macros

Any task in Excel may be performed by a "macro". Macros typically carry out simple but repetitive tasks, such as entering your name and address. Macros may also be used for complex tasks that are difficult to reproduce accurately without some kind of help.

To create a macro, carry out an example of the actions with Excel recording the keystrokes involved as you complete the task. The sequence is stored as a macro in the **Visual Basic for Applications** (VBA) programming language. You can edit your recorded macro or create new macros using the Visual Basic Editor.

Macros can be very powerful, because they can run commands on your computer. For this reason, Excel prevents the default Excel file format (file type **.xlsx**) from storing VBA macro code. The recommended place for storing your macros is in a hidden **Personal Macro Workbook**, and this is the method used for the examples on the following pages. If you share macros, they need to be stored in the workbooks that use them. These workbooks must then be saved in the Excel macro-enabled file format (file type **.xlsm**). You may need to reset the security level temporarily to enable all macros so that you can edit macros in the active workbook:

Beware

Macros are powerful, but can be subject to misuse. Microsoft has therefore included security checks and limitations in Excel to help prevent them from being introduced into your system maliciously.

1 Select the **File** tab, **Options**, **Trust Center**, then click the **Trust Center Settings...** button

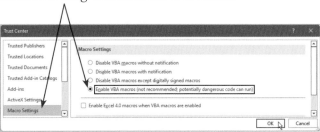

2 Select **Macro Settings**, then check the **Enable VBA Macros** setting and click the **OK** button

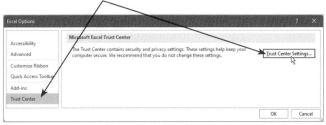

Enable VBA Macros is not recommended as a permanent setting. Select a restricted level when you have finished creating or changing the macros stored in your active workbook.

Create Macros

To display the commands for recording and viewing macros:

1 Select the **View** tab, and click the arrow below the **Macros** button, in the [**Macros**] group

2 You can choose to view or record macros, and choose between relative or absolute cell references (this is a toggle setting)

These options are also available from the **Developer** tab, along with the **Macro Security** and **Visual Basic** commands. By default, this tab is not displayed. To add the **Developer** tab to the Ribbon:

1 Click the **File** tab, then select **Options** (or press the **Alt + F – T** keys) and choose **Customize Ribbon**

2 Check the **Developer** box in the **Main Tabs** section, then click **OK** to add the **Developer** tab to the Ribbon

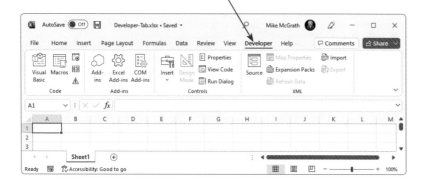

Selecting the **Macros** button rather than the arrow has the same effect as selecting the **View Macros** entry.

141

You can record, view, and edit macros, using commands from either the **View** tab or the **Developer** tab, but to create macros from scratch or to change security settings, you will need to use the **Developer** tab.

Record a Macro

Assume that you need to add some standard disclaimer text to a number of workbooks. To create a macro for this:

1 Open a blank workbook, then click in cell **A1**

2 Select the **Developer** tab, [**Code**] group, **Use Relative References** button, then click the **Record Macro** button – to open a "Record Macro" dialog box

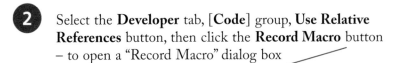

3 Enter a name for the macro, and specify a shortcut key – e.g. **Shift + D** (the **Ctrl** key gets prefixed automatically)

4 Select **Personal Macro Workbook** (the preferred location to store macros), add a description, then click **OK** to start the recording

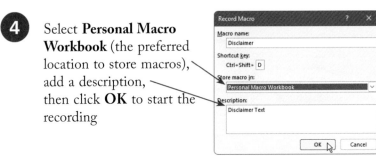

5 Carry out the required actions (for example, type some text in the cells), then select the **Developer** tab and from the [**Code**] group click the **Stop Recording** button

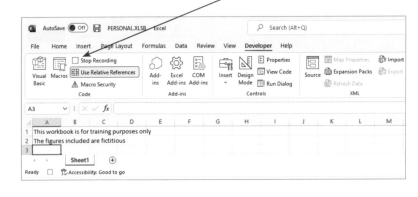

To check out the macro:

1 Click in a different cell (**C4**, for example), then press the **Ctrl** + **Shift** + **D** shortcut to try out the macro

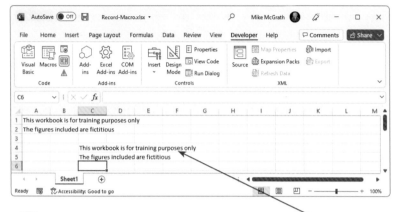

Don't forget

If there are problems with the macro, you may be able to use the **Visual Basic Editor** to make the changes that are needed (see page 148).

2 The text is entered into the worksheet in the active cell

The start location changes because the macro was created with relative references. However, if you click in any specific cells while the macro is being recorded, those references will be honored.

When you have finished checking the macro, close the workbook:

1 Click the **File** tab, and select **Close**

2 Select **Don't Save** when asked if you want to save your changes

Beware

The relative reference applies to the macro, as the initial cell was selected before macro recording was started.

The macro itself will be retained in the **Personal Macro Workbook**. This will be saved at the end of the Excel session (see page 144).

Active Workbook Macros

If you prefer to store the recorded macro in the active workbook, you must save that workbook as file type **.xlsm**. You will also need to reset the level of macro security (see page 140). When you close the active workbook the macros it contains are no longer available in that Excel session, unless you save it – as described on page 144.

Apply the Macro

1 Open a workbook that requires the disclaimer text, and select the location (e.g. **My Personal Budget**, cell **A16**)

The macro remains available throughout the Excel session if you stored it in the **Personal Macro Workbook**, and you can apply it to any Excel workbook (**.xlsm**, **.xlsx**, or **.xls**). Once saved, it will be available to use in future sessions.

The workbook type does not need to be changed to **.xlsm** as it has added text, not macro code.

If you choose not to save in the **Personal Macro Workbook**, any macros created during this Excel session will be lost. This can be a useful way of trying out new ideas, without commitment.

2 Press the **Ctrl** + **Shift** + **D** shortcut to run the macro

3 Save the worksheet (no need to change the file type)

4 When you end the Excel session, you can save your **Personal Macro Workbook** and with it, any macros that you have created during the session

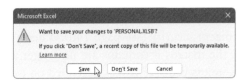

View the Macro

1 Select the **View** tab, then from the [**Window**] group, click the **Unhide** button

2 Select the "PERSONAL. XLSB" workbook, which is your **Personal Macro Workbook**, then click **OK**

3 Click the **Developer** tab and from the [**Code**] group, select **Macros**

4 Select the macro you want to review

5 Click the **Edit** button to display the code in the **Visual Basic Editor**

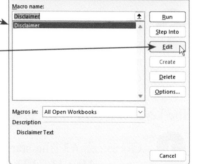

6 Select **File**, **Save PERSONAL.XLSB** to save any changes, then click **Close and Return to Microsoft Excel**

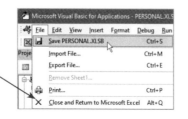

Don't forget

You can view and edit a macro. However, since it is stored in a hidden workbook, you must start by making the workbook visible.

Hot tip

You can make changes to a macro – e.g. revise the text that is entered into the cells – even if you don't know the VBA language.

Beware

When you've finished viewing or changing your macros, you should select **View**, **Hide** to hide the **Personal Macro Workbook**.

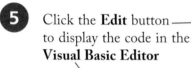

Macro to Make a Table

1 Open a **Share history** file – "META.csv", for example

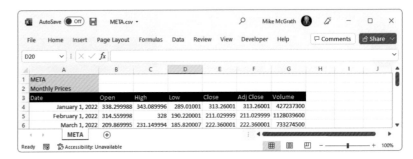

Hot tip

You can record a macro that carries out a more complex task – creating an Excel Table from a **Share history** file, for example.

2 Select **Developer**, [**Code**], **Use Relative References**, then click **Record Macro**

3 Specify the macro name, shortcut key combination and description, then click **OK** to start recording

The keystroke steps in the process are as follows:

1 Go to cell **A3** (the start of the data range):
   Alt + H – FD – G, A3 then **Enter**

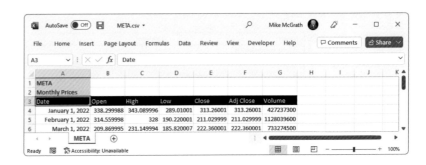

Hot tip

You may find that it is better to use keystrokes rather than mouse selections when creating a macro. It is also useful to carry out a practice run, noting the keystrokes required, and then record the macro.

2 Select the whole data range using the arrow keys:
   Shift + Down arrow
   Ctrl + Shift + Right arrow
   Ctrl + Shift + Down arrow

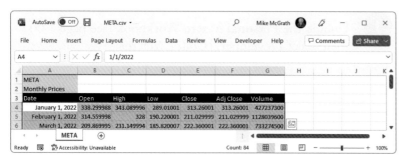

This shows the data range selected, ready for creating an Excel Table.

3 Create an Excel Table from the selected set of data:——————
$\quad$ **Alt + N – T**, then **Enter**

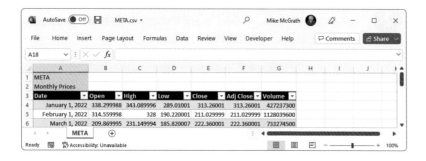

If the data column is in descending order, it may be unsuitable for a lookup table.

In some cases, **Share history** files are in descending sequence. To ensure ascending sequence, add these keystrokes:

4 Go to cell **A4** (the date field in the first row of actual data):
$\quad$ **Alt + H – FD – G, A4** then **Enter**

5 Sort the column in ascending date sequence:
$\quad$ **Alt + A – SA**

6 Click **Developer, [Code], Stop Recording** to finish the macro, then save the table as an Excel Workbook in **.xlsx** format

If you create an Excel Table in a **.csv** file, you must save as an Excel Workbook (**.xlsx** format), to retain the table (see page 149).

Edit the Macro

1 Unhide the **Personal Macro Workbook** (see page 145), then select **Developer**, **[Code]**, **Macros**

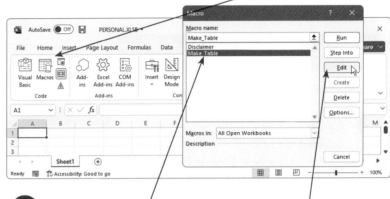

Check the recorded macro to see if any changes are needed.

2 Select the "Make_Table" macro, then click **Edit** to display the code in the **Visual Basic Editor**

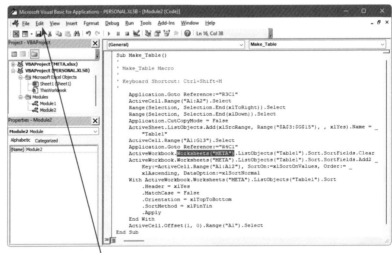

You should hide the **Personal Macro Workbook** when you have finished making changes to the macro.

Sections of the macro may be specific to the original workbook. In this case, there are references to the worksheet name. These can be replaced with the generic reference to **ActiveSheet**.

3 Select **Edit**, **Replace**, and **Find** the text "Worksheets("META")", click **Replace With** "ActiveSheet" then click **Replace All**

4 To save the changes, select **File**, **Save PERSONAL.XLSB**, then select **File**, **Close and Return to Microsoft Excel**

Use the Macro

1 Open another **Share history** file – "NFLX.csv", for example

This example has the data in descending sequence:

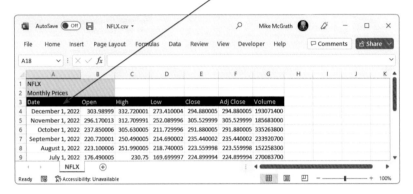

2 Press the **Ctrl** + **Shift** + **M** macro shortcut key to create an Excel Table (with the data in ascending sequence)

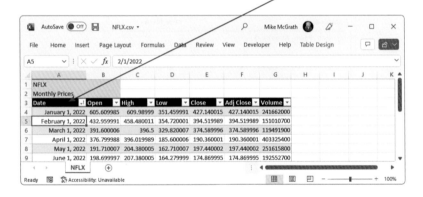

3 Save the worksheet as file type **Excel Workbook (.xlsx)**

Repeat this for any other **Share history** files, which can each be converted to Excel Table format with a single click of the "Make_Table" macro shortcut key.

Follow a similar procedure to create and test macros for any other tasks that you need to complete on a regular basis.

Beware

As written, the macro assumes that the worksheet will have data in rows 4 to 15 (January 2022-December 2022). If there are fewer actual rows, the remainder will appear as empty table rows. Extra rows will be stored after the table.

Hot tip

The macro now refers to the **ActiveSheet**, so it converts the data range in the current worksheet, without regard to its name.

Don't forget

The macro remains in the **Personal Macro Workbook**, so the shared workbooks do not need to be macro-enabled.

Create Macros with VBA

Hot tip

A list of album tracks is used here to illustrate the use of Visual Basic to create a macro; in this case, to insert page breaks after each album.

Don't forget

This macro identifies the last non-blank row in the worksheet. It checks the values in column 4 (Album), and inserts a page break whenever the name changes.

Hot tip

You can discover more about Visual Basic programming in our companion books, **Excel VBA in easy steps** and **Visual Basic in easy steps**.

1 Select the **Developer** tab, [**Code**], **Visual Basic**

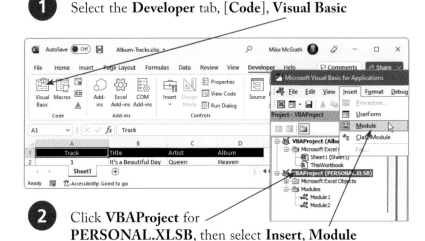

2 Click **VBAProject** for PERSONAL.XLSB, then select **Insert, Module**

3 In the module code window, type (or paste) the macro code

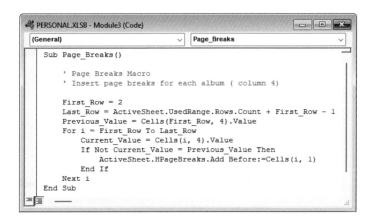

```
Sub Page_Breaks()

    ' Page Breaks Macro
    ' Insert page breaks for each album ( column 4)

    First_Row = 2
    Last_Row = ActiveSheet.UsedRange.Rows.Count + First_Row - 1
    Previous_Value = Cells(First_Row, 4).Value
    For i = First_Row To Last_Row
        Current_Value = Cells(i, 4).Value
        If Not Current_Value = Previous_Value Then
            ActiveSheet.HPageBreaks.Add Before:=Cells(i, 1)
        End If
    Next i
End Sub
```

4 When you have entered and checked the macro code, select **File, Close and Return to Microsoft Excel**

Visit **docs.microsoft.com/samples** for sample Visual Basic macros.

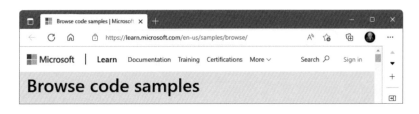

...cont'd

5 In the worksheet, click the **Page Break Preview** button on the status bar to see the page setup

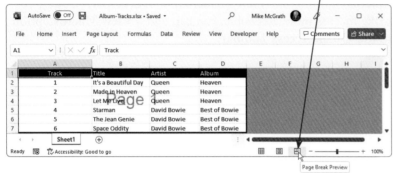

Here, the second album continues on the same page as the first. To apply page breaks based on albums:

1 Click **Developer**, **[Code]**, **Macros**

2 Select the "Page_Breaks" macro, then click **Run**

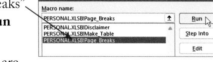

3 Manual page breaks are inserted at every change of album in the worksheet

151

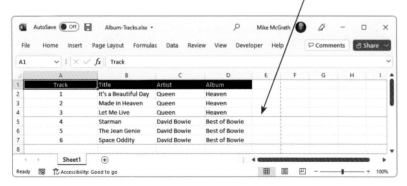

4 Select **Page Layout**, **[Page Setup]**, **Print Titles**

5 Set **Rows to repeat at top** to the first row so that you get the headings on every print page

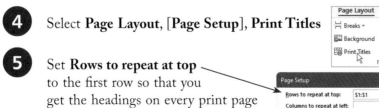

Add Macros to the Toolbar

If you specified a **Ctrl** or **Shift** + **Ctrl** shortcut when you created your macro, you can run the macro by pressing the appropriate key combination. You can also run the macro by clicking the **Macros** button from **View**, [**Macros**] or **Developer**, [**Code**]. To make macros more accessible, you can add a **View Macros** option to the **Quick Access Toolbar**:

1 Select **File**, **Options** and select **Quick Access Toolbar**, then choose **All Commands** in **Choose commands from**

Hot tip

You could also right-click the **Macros** button and select **Add to Quick Access Toolbar**.

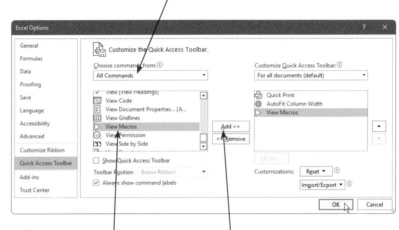

2 Click **View Macros**, click **Add**, and click **OK**. See that **View Macros** now appears on the **Quick Access Toolbar**

Don't forget

If you want to add or change the shortcut key for a macro, select it by using the **Macros** button, and then click the **Options** button.

3 To run a macro, click the **View Macros** button on the **Quick Access Toolbar**, then select the macro you want, and click **Run**

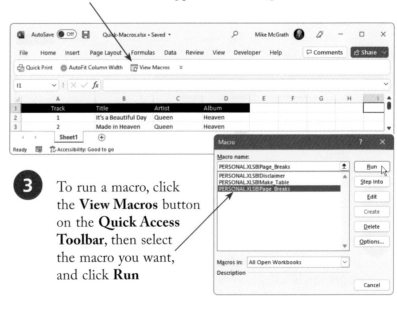

...cont'd

Alternatively, you can add specific macros as individual icons on the **Quick Access Toolbar**. To do this:

1 Open **File**, **Options**, select **Quick Access Toolbar**, then choose **Macros** in **Choose commands from**

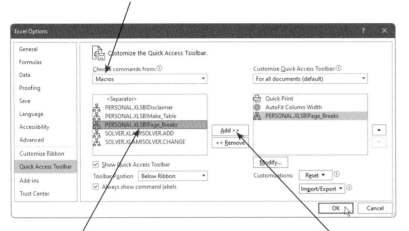

Macros can also be associated with graphics or hotspots on the worksheet.

2 Select the particular macro you want, then click **Add**

3 Each macro will have the same icon, but you can click the **Modify** button in the "Excel Options" dialog and select a different icon ——

4 The selected macro will be added to the **Quick Access Toolbar**

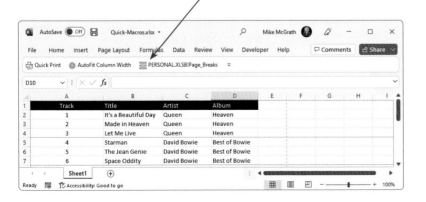

Simply click an individual macro on the **Quick Access Toolbar** to instantly run that macro.

153

Debug Macros

If you are having a problem with a macro, or if you are just curious to see how it works, you can run it one step at a time:

1 Select **Macros** from **Developer**, [**Code**] or from **View**, [**Macros**], then choose the macro you want to run, and click **Step Into**

2 Press **F8** repeatedly to run through the code, one step at a time

Open a worksheet for which the macro was written, before selecting the **Step Into** option.

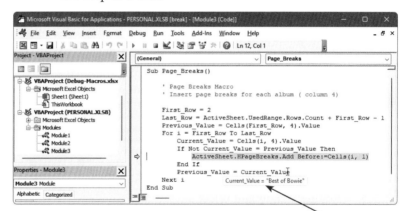

3 At any stage, hold the mouse over any variable to see its current value

4 Select the **Debug** menu to see other testing options such as **Step Over** and **Step Out**

Debug	Run	Tools	Add-Ins	Window
Compile VBAProject				
Step Into				F8
Step Over				Shift+F8
Step Out				Ctrl+Shift+F8
Run To Cursor				Ctrl+F8
Add Watch...				
Edit Watch...				Ctrl+W
Quick Watch...				Shift+F9
Toggle Breakpoint				F9
Clear All Breakpoints				Ctrl+Shift+F9
Set Next Statement				Ctrl+F9
Show Next Statement				

A breakpoint is the macro statement at which execution will automatically stop. The breakpoints you set will not be saved with the code when you exit.

5 Click in the margin to add breakpoints, then press **F5** to continue to the next breakpoint (or exit the macro if no breakpoints are set)

6 To finish and leave **Debug**, select **File**, **Close and Return to Microsoft Excel**

10 Templates and Scenarios

For the most frequent uses of Excel, you'll find ready-made templates to give you a head start. There are more Excel resources at Microsoft Office Support and other websites. Excel also has special problem-solving tools.

Templates

You can save effort, and you may discover new aspects of Excel, if you base your new workbooks on available templates.

1 Click the **File** tab, then click **New** to be offered the blank workbook and also see suggestions for templates

2 Review the example templates, or select a category such as "Planners and Trackers" to see more templates

Hot tip

You can also search for and select templates from the Start screen that normally displays when you start Excel.

3 Select a template to use – "Loan Amortization Schedule", for example – then review the details and click **Create**

Don't forget

The template will be downloaded and a workbook will be opened ready for use, though you can make any changes you wish, if it doesn't exactly meet your requirements.

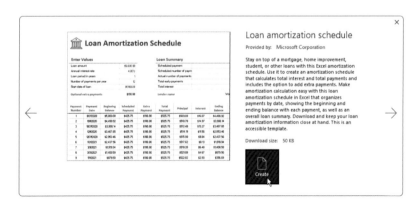

4 The input boxes are predefined with data, so you can discover the way the workbook operates

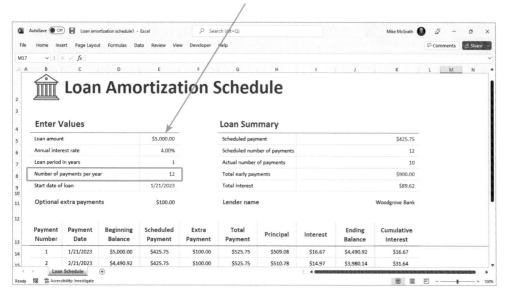

5 Adjust the values, and the worksheet is extended by the number of payments and displays the calculated amounts

6 To see the formulas behind the calculations, press **Ctrl + `** (or select **Formulas**, [**Formula Auditing**], **Show Formulas**)

7 Select **Formulas**, [**Defined Names**], **Name Manager** to see the names defined in the workbook, with their values and cell references

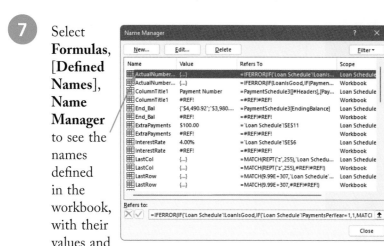

Hot tip

Review the data and then make changes to the values to see the effect. For example, change the payments per year from 12 to 6.

Don't forget

To keep the results, you need to save the workbook – the default name is the template name with a number appended.

Online Templates

To help in creating a workbook for a particular purpose, you can amend an existing template and save the revised copy in your **Custom Office Templates** library for later use.

1 Select **File**, **New** and click **Search for online templates**. Enter a term (e.g. "exercise"), then click the **Search** button

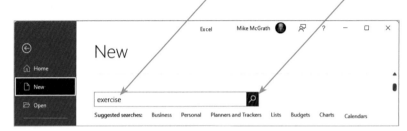

2 Thumbnail images of matching templates will be listed

3 Scroll down, and you will see that related templates from your other Microsoft 365 Office apps may also be detected

Don't forget

The last template that you downloaded and used will be listed in the featured templates ready for possible re-use.

Hot tip

The templates may be in compatibility mode if they were originally designed for a previous version of Excel.

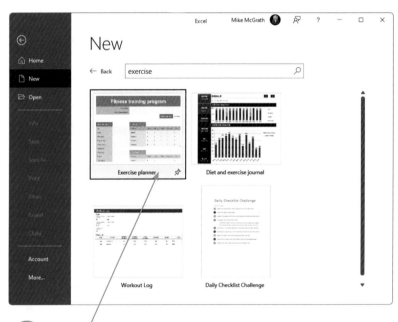

4 Choose a template, and create a new workbook (see page 156)

...cont'd

You can amend the selected template and save the revised copy in your **Documents\Custom Office Templates** library for later use.

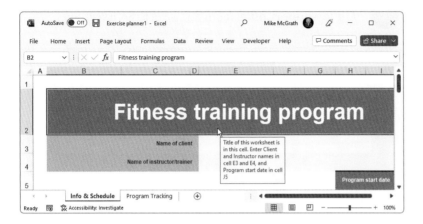

159

1. Select **File, Save As**, then select your **Documents\Custom Office Templates** folder and choose the **Excel Template (*.xltx)** file type

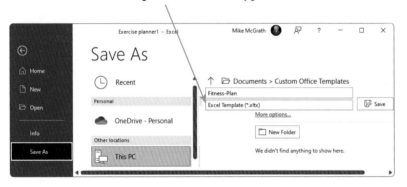

Hot tip

If the template contains macros or Visual Basic code, you will need to save it as an **Excel Macro-Enabled Template (*.xltm)**.

2. Select **File, New, Personal** to view your templates

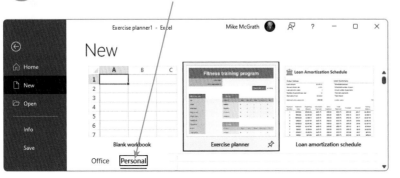

Don't forget

You can also save an Excel Workbook as a template to use as the basis for other workbooks. Such templates are also saved in the **Personal** area.

More Excel Resources

The internet is a prolific source of advice and guidance for Excel users at all levels. Here are some websites that may prove useful:

1 Go to **support.office.com** and select the **Excel** icon

Don't forget

A search on **google.com** with Excel-related search terms will result in millions of matches, so it will be easier to start from a more focused website such as Microsoft Office Support.

2 Select a topic, such as "Formulas & functions", then choose an item, such as "Overview of formulas in Excel"

Beware

The actual links and content for the Office web pages change over time, but you should expect to find links similar to those shown.

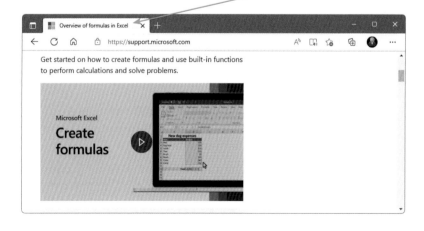

...cont'd

3 Microsoft MVPs (most valued professionals) can also provide useful information. Go to **mvp.microsoft.com**

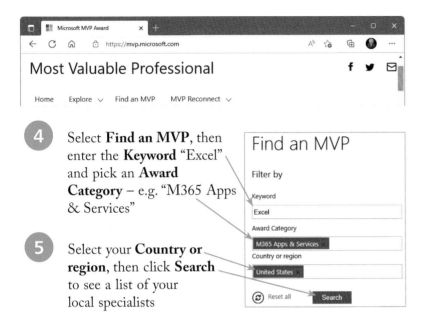

There is every possibility that your Excel question may have been answered previously on the community forum – use the Search box before repeating the question.

4 Select **Find an MVP**, then enter the **Keyword** "Excel" and pick an **Award Category** – e.g. "M365 Apps & Services"

5 Select your **Country or region**, then click **Search** to see a list of your local specialists

If you are interested in creating Excel functions and macros, you should visit the Office and Excel developers' center:

6 Go to **developer.microsoft.com/office** and select **Build applications for Excel,** then click **Learn more**

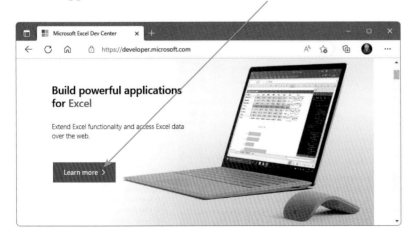

You'll find that many forum references relate to previous versions of Excel, but these will often be just as applicable to the latest version of Excel.

What-If Analysis

A **What-If Analysis** involves the process of changing values in cells to see how those changes affect the outcome on a worksheet. A set of values that represent a particular outcome is known as a "scenario". To create a scenario:

1 Download then open the **Simple loan calculator** template, and enter details for a loan – for example a 25-year mortgage, for $250,000 at an interest rate of 7.95%

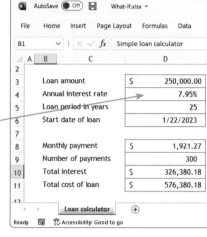

Sometimes you can set up your worksheet so that several outcomes are visible at once (as on page 93). You can get a similar effect by using a **What-If Analysis**, and defining scenarios.

162

2 Select the **Data** tab and, from the [**Forecast**] group, click **What-If Analysis**, then choose **Scenario Manager...**

3 Click **Add**, type a scenario name (e.g. "X001"), enter the address references for cells that you may want to change (e.g. loan amount and period), then click **OK**

You can create a new worksheet to forecast data trends using the **Forecast Sheet** option in the **Data** tab's [**Forecast**] group.

In this case, the chosen cells in this scenario can explore the effects of changing the loan amount and the loan repayment term.

4 Change the value for the loan to a lesser amount in this scenario, then click **OK**

...cont'd

5 Repeat steps 3 and 4 for each scenario, clicking **Add** then **OK**, incrementing each name by 1 (i.e. "X002", "X003", etc.)

6 When you've specified the last scenario, click **OK** to complete the process

7 Select one of the scenarios (e.g. "X001" – a lesser loan amount), then click **Show** to display the associated results on the worksheet

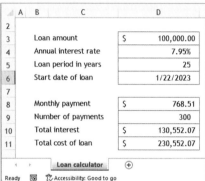

In the Scenario Manager you can click **Edit** to make changes or corrections to a scenario, or click **Delete** if you no longer want the selected scenario.

8 Select another scenario (e.g. "X002" – a lesser loan amount _and_ a shorter loan period), then click **Show** to display the associated results on the worksheet

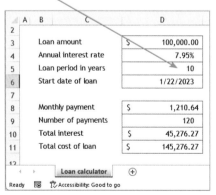

The date of creation or modification is recorded in the Scenario Manager **Comments**.

The last scenario results will be displayed in the worksheet, or the original worksheet values will be shown if no scenario is selected.

Summary Reports

To create a scenario summary report, showing all the possible outcomes on one worksheet:

1 On the **Data** tab, in the [**Forecast**] group, click **What-If Analysis**, and select **Scenario Manager**, then click the **Summary...** button

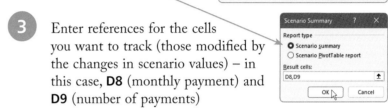

2 Choose the **Scenario summary** report type

3 Enter references for the cells you want to track (those modified by the changes in scenario values) – in this case, **D8** (monthly payment) and **D9** (number of payments)

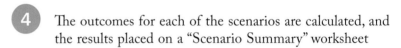

4 The outcomes for each of the scenarios are calculated, and the results placed on a "Scenario Summary" worksheet

In the "Scenario Summary" worksheet, the values for the selected scenario appear in the **Changing Cells** section.

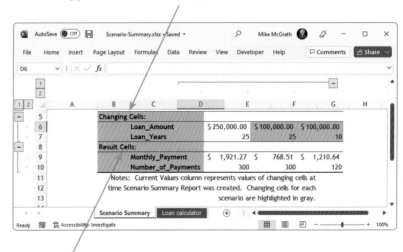

The **Result Cells** section shows the monthly payments and number of payments for the selected scenario.

The results can also be presented as a **Scenario PivotTable** report:

1 Open the **Scenario Manager**, click **Summary**, choose **Scenario PivotTable report**, and enter the references for the result cells (number of payments and total interest)

2 The results are shown in a table on a separate worksheet

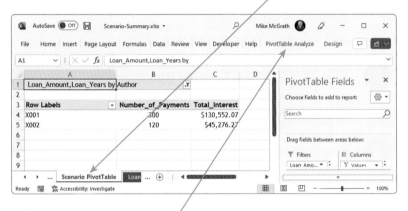

3 Select the **PivotTable Analyze** tab and click **PivotChart** in the [**Tools**] group

4 Choose the type of chart (**3-D Stacked Column**, for example), then click **OK**

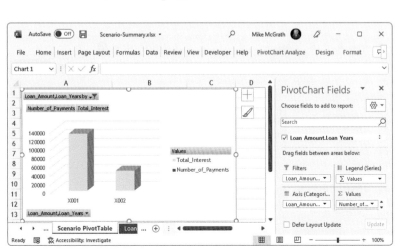

Beware

You must switch back to the **Loan calculator** worksheet before opening the **Scenario Manager**.

Hot tip

To generate a **Scenario PivotTable** report, it is always necessary to specify the relevant result cells you desire.

165

Don't forget

You can change the chart definition to suit the ranges of data displayed. As with any chart, you can select **Design**, **Location**, **Move Chart**, and place the **PivotChart** on a separate worksheet.

Goal Seek

If you know the result that you want from an analysis, but not the input values the worksheet needs to get that result, you can use the **Goal Seek** feature. For example, you can use **Goal Seek** in the "Loan Calculator" worksheet to see how much you could borrow if you could only afford monthly payments of $1,000:

1 Select **Data, What-If Analysis** from the [**Forecast**] group, then choose **Goal Seek...**

2 For **Set cell**, enter the cell with the value you want to change (cell **D8**, your "Monthly payment")

Start off with the original data scenario, and the extra payment value will be incremented until the target interest level has been achieved.

3 In the box for **To value**, type the value you want to apply (your affordable monthly payment amount of $1,000)

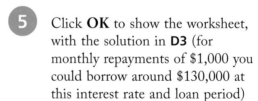

4 In the box for **By changing cell**, enter the cell containing the value you want to adjust to suit your monthly payment (**D3**, available "Loan amount")

The **By changing cell** value must be referred to by the formula in the **Set cell** field, where the changes should be reflected.

5 Click **OK** to show the worksheet, with the solution in **D3** (for monthly repayments of $1,000 you could borrow around $130,000 at this interest rate and loan period)

The references for the **Set cell** field and for the **By changing cell** field must be to single cells only.

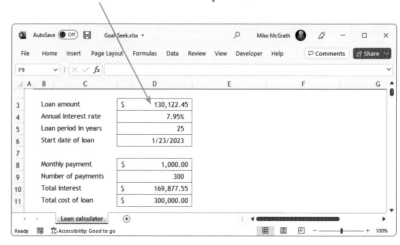

Optimization

Goal Seek allows you to solve problems where you want to find the value of a single input to generate the desired result. It is of no help when you need to find the best values for several inputs. For this, you require an optimizer – a software tool that helps you find the best way to allocate resources. These could be raw materials, machine time, people time, money, or anything that is in limited supply. The best or optimal solution will perhaps be the one that maximizes profit, minimizes cost, or meets some other requirement. All kinds of situations can be tackled in this way, including allocating finance, scheduling production, blending raw materials, routing goods, and loading transportation.

Excel includes an **Add-in** optimizer, called **Solver**. You may need to install this (see page 103) if it doesn't appear on your system. To illustrate **Solver**, we'll examine a product mix problem.

Sample Solver Problem

Imagine that your hobby is textiles, and that you produce craft goods (ponchos, scarves, and gloves). There's a craft fair coming up, and you plan to use your existing inventory of materials (warp, weft, and braid) and your available time (for the loom, and to finish goods). You want to know the mix of products that will maximize profits, given the inventory and time available. These include 800 hanks of warp, 600 hanks of weft, 50 lengths of braid, 300 hours of loom time, and 200 hours of finishing time.

To produce a poncho, you will need 8 units of warp, 7 of weft, 1 of braid, 6 for loom, and 2 for finish. For a scarf, the values are 3 warp, 2 weft, 0 braid, 1 loom, and 1 finish. For a pair of gloves, they are 1 warp, 0 weft, 0 braid, 0 loom, and 4 finish.

You make the assumption that your profit is $25 per poncho, $10 per scarf, and $8 per pair of gloves.

You remember that you need four of each item as samples to show the visitors to the fair. Also, you recall that usually, half the scarves are sold in sets with gloves.

Relationships between the objective, constraints, and decision variables are analyzed to decide the best solution, to satisfy the requirements.

The problem description must be in sufficient detail to establish relationships and identify constraints.

Project Worksheet

The craft fair optimization information (see page 167) can be expressed in the following worksheet, with the underlying formulas also displayed:

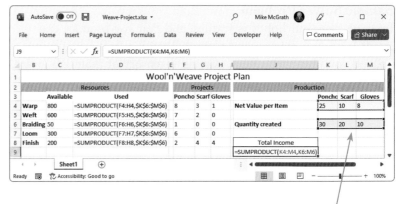

Hot tip

The worksheet captures information about resources available, and the amounts needed for any specified level of production.

Don't forget

Some constraints are specified in the problem description, while others may be implicit – e.g. the requirement for integer (and positive) values of production.

Sample values for the production quantities have been inserted, just to check that the worksheet operates as expected. Excel **Solver** can be used to compute the optimum quantities. These are limitations or constraints that could be taken into account:

- The number of available resources cannot be exceeded.

- There must be at least four of each product (samples for the craft show).

- There must be whole numbers of products (integers).

- There must be a pair of gloves each for at least half the scarves (so that sets can be offered for sale).

Solver

To calculate the optimum solution for the craft fair problem:

1 Click the cell **J9**, which contains the target value for "Total Income", then select the **Data** tab, and click **Solver** in the [**Analyze**] group

Solver will use the currently-selected cell as the target, unless you replace this reference with another cell.

2 Check the **Max** option, then click the **By Changing Variable Cells** box to select it

3 Use the ⬆ collapse/expand button to select product quantity cells (**K6:M6**), then click **Add**

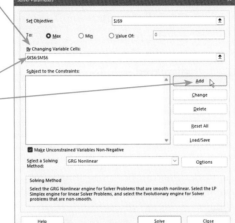

4 Select cells to specify that resources used must be <u>less than</u> or equal to (**<=**) those available, then click the **Add** button

Click **Add** to define the next constraint, or click **OK** to return to the "**Solver Parameters**" dialog box.

5 Select cells that indicate the quantities created, and specify these must be <u>greater than</u> or equal to (**>=**) 4, then click the **Add** button

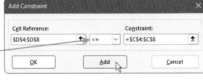

6 Create a constraint that the quantities created must be integers (**Int**), then click the **Add** button

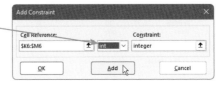

...cont'd

7 Ensure the quantity of gloves must be at least half that of scarves, then click **OK**

8 Review the list of constraints in the "Solver Parameters" dialog. Click **Solve** to see the results calculated and displayed

Hot tip

Check the box to make all unconstrained variables non-negative.

Hot tip

The **Answer Report** worksheet added each time you run **Solver** will show detailed results and the constraints that have been applied. Click **Save Scenario** to keep a record of the settings.

9 If **Solver** finds a solution, click **Keep Solver Solution**, clear **Return to Solver Parameters Dialog**, then click **OK** to return to the workbook

		Resources		Projects				Production		
		Available	Used	Poncho	Scarf	Gloves		Poncho	Scarf	Gloves
Warp		800	457	8	3	1	Net Value per Item	25	10	8
Weft		600	382	7	2	0				
Braiding		50	50	1	0	0	Quantity created	50	16	9
Loom		300	300	6	0	0				
Finish		200	200	2	4	4	Total Income			
							$1,482			

11 Links and Connections

Excel lets you make external references to other workbooks or to web pages that contain data needed for your active worksheet. Your worksheet is updated automatically if the source data changes. You can also share your data as a Microsoft 365 Office document, or as a PDF.

Link to Workbooks

Sometimes, you may want to refer to the data in one workbook from another separate workbook. You may, for example, want to provide an alternative view of the data in a worksheet, or to merge data from individual workbooks to create a summary workbook. You can refer to the contents of cells in another workbook by creating external references (also known as "links").

References may be to a cell or to a range, though it is usually better to refer to a defined name in the other workbook.

To establish defined names in a source workbook:

1 Open a source workbook – **North.xlsx**, for example

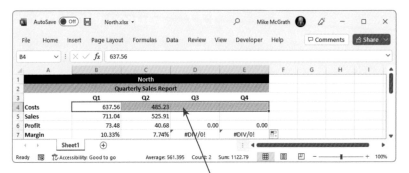

Don't forget

This shows the sales by quarter for one region with the first two quarters entered. The calculations for margin (profit/sales) for the remaining quarters show zero divide errors, since the associated sales values are zero.

2 Select a range of cells – **B4:E4** (the costs, for example)

3 Select the **Formulas** tab, then click **Define Name**, from the [**Defined Names**] group

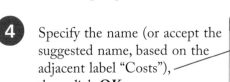

4 Specify the name (or accept the suggested name, based on the adjacent label "Costs"), then click **OK**

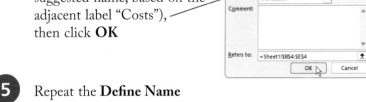

Hot tip

Workbook links are very useful when you need to combine information from several workbooks that may be created in different locations or on different systems.

5 Repeat the **Define Name** process for "Sales" values (cells **B5:E5**) and for "Profit" values (cells **B6:E6**)

6 Select the **Formulas** tab and click **Name Manager**, in the [**Defined Names**] group, to see all the name definitions

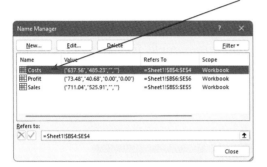

Hot tip

The benefit of links is that when source workbooks change, you won't have to make changes manually to the destination workbooks that refer to those sources.

7 Save and close the workbook to record the names

8 Repeat this for each of the other source workbooks ("South", "East", and "West") in turn, defining range names "Costs", "Sales", and "Profit" for each one

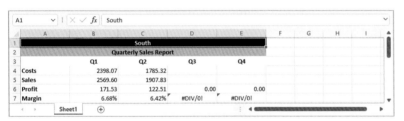

Don't forget

The names will have the same cell references for the associated ranges as those shown for the "**North**" workbook.

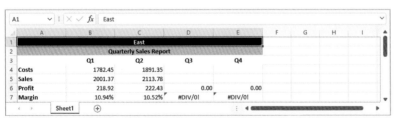

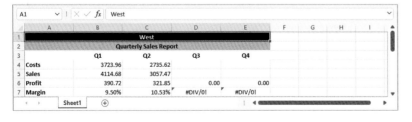

9 Save and close each workbook to record the names

173

Create External References

1 Open the source workbooks that contain the cells you want to refer to (e.g. "North", "South", "East", "West")

2 Open the workbook that will contain the external references (in this example, it's named **Overall.xlsx**)

Hot tip

You can incorporate an external reference into a function or formula, as you might with any cell reference.

3 Select the cell in which you want to create the first of the external references (e.g. **B4**) and type (for example) **=SUM(**

4 Select the **View** tab and, in the [**Windows**] group, click **Switch Windows**, then click the source workbook to make it active (if necessary, select the worksheet with the cells that you want to link to)

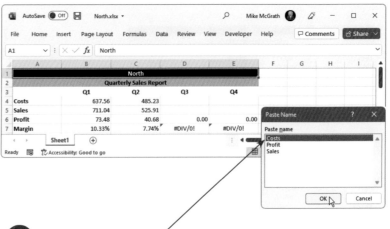

Don't forget

When you paste **Costs** into the **Overall** worksheet it is the total costs from the **North** worksheet **Costs** row (i.e. Q1 plus Q2).

5 Press **F3**, and select the defined name for the range of cells – e.g. "Costs", then click **OK** and press **Enter**

6 Similarly, enter a formula in **B5** to sum "Sales", and enter a formula in **B6** to sum "Profit"

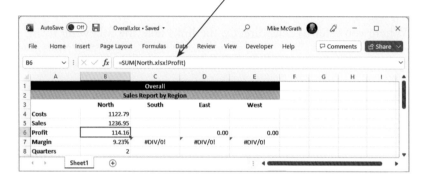

7 You can also refer to source workbook cells directly. Click in cell **B8**, and type **=COUNT(**

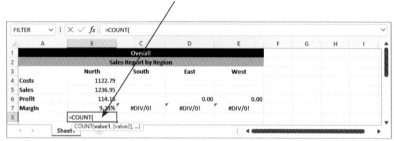

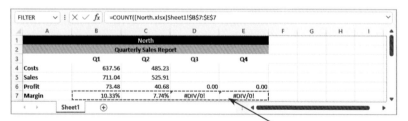

8 Switch to "North", and select the cell range **B7:E7**, then press **Enter** to complete the cell reference and formula

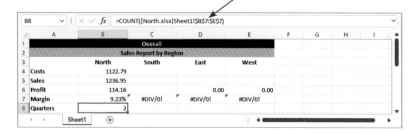

Styles of Reference

While the source workbooks are open, the links to defined names take the following form:

North.xlsx!Costs

Where you refer to cells directly, the links take the following form:

[North.xlsx]Sheet1!$B$7:$E$7

Note that the cell references could be relative or mixed, as well as absolute, as shown.

Close the source workbook and you'll find that the external references are immediately expanded to include a fully-qualified link to the source workbook file with file path and defined name:

Quotation marks will be applied to the workbook name, if it contains any spaces – for example, **'The North.xlsx'!Costs**.

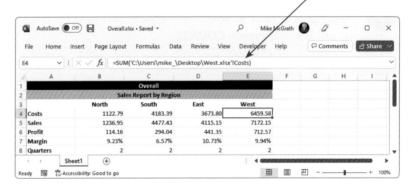

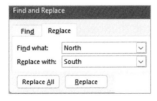

Hot tip

The references for **South**, **East**, and **West** have been incorporated. You can do this via a selection, as with **North**, or you can just copy the formulas for **North** and change the name appropriately.

Find and Replace		
Find	Replace	
Find what:	North	
Replace with:	South	
Replace All	Replace	

Links with direct cell references also show the fully-qualified link, with file path and cell names:

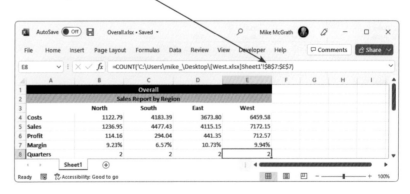

In each case, the path, file name and worksheet name will be enclosed in quote marks, whether there are spaces included or not.

Source Workbook Changes

Assume that you receive new versions of the source workbooks (containing the next quarter's data). You can control how and when these changes affect the destination workbook:

1 Open the destination workbook **(Overall.xlsx)**

2 By default you'll receive a warning message saying there are external links, and offering an option to apply updates

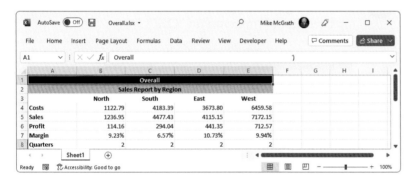

3 Select **Don't Update**, to open the workbook unchanged

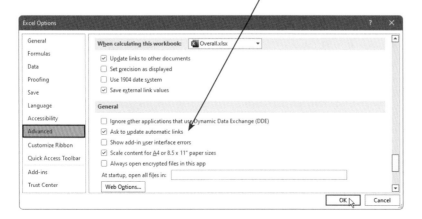

4 Select **File, Options**, then click **Advanced** and review the **General** settings – e.g. **Ask to update automatic links**

Don't forget

Leave source workbooks closed. When source and destination workbooks are open at the same time on the same computer, links will be updated automatically.

Hot tip

Select **Update** and the source workbooks will be accessed and any changes will be applied when the destination workbook opens.

Beware

Do not use this option to turn off the prompt, or you will not be aware when workbooks get updated. Use the workbook-specific option (see page 179) instead.

Apply Updates

1 Select the **Data** tab, then, in the [**Queries & Connections**] group, choose the **Edit Links** command

2 Select links to refresh, then click **Update Values**

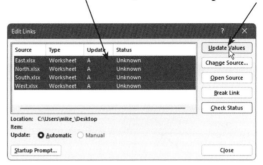

Don't forget

You can also update only selected entries and use the **Check Status** button to see which entries are not applied.

3 Data changes are applied, and the worksheet status is updated from "Unknown" to "OK"

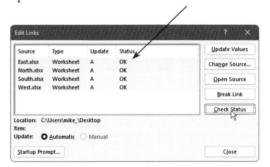

Beware

Do not apply updates where you are unsure of the origin of the changes, or if you want to retain current values.

4 The updated information is added to the destination workbook, which now displays the data for <u>three</u> quarters

Hot tip

To see trends in **Costs**, select cell **F4**, click **Insert**, pick a **Sparklines** type and select data range (**B4:E4**). Copy **F4** to **F5:F7** to see trends in **Sales**, **Profit**, and **Margins**.

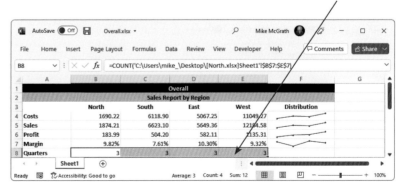

178

Turn Off the Prompt

If you are confident with the integrity of external links, you can turn off the update prompt for a specific workbook. To do this:

1 Open the workbook and select **Edit Links** from the [**Queries & Connections**] group on the **Data** tab

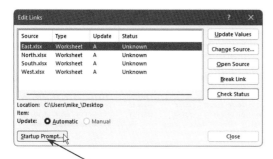

2 Click the **Startup Prompt...** button and choose **Don't display the alert and update links**, then click **OK**

Don't forget

If you choose **Don't display the alert and don't update automatic links**, users of the workbook won't be aware when the data in the workbook becomes out of date.

3 Whenever you open that workbook in future, Excel will automatically check for updates and apply the latest values from the source workbooks

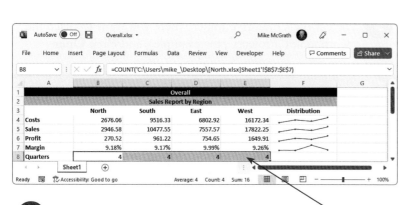

Hot tip

This shows the effect when you open the destination workbook after updates have been applied to the source workbooks.

4 The "Overall" workbook now displays data for <u>four</u> quarters

Save Workbook Online

You can store workbooks and other documents online, and access them via Microsoft 365 Online apps or share them with other users. To copy a workbook to OneDrive from within Excel:

1 Open a workbook, click the **File** tab, and select **Save As**

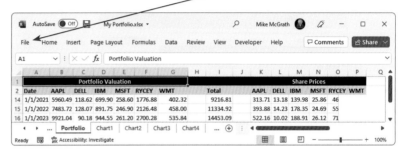

2 Select the OneDrive for the current user and click **More options...** to explore the OneDrive contents

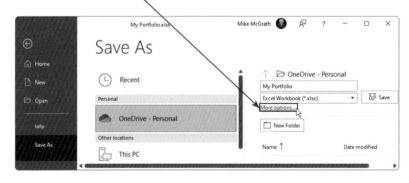

3 Select the OneDrive folder where you want to place the workbook ("Projects", for example), and click **Open**

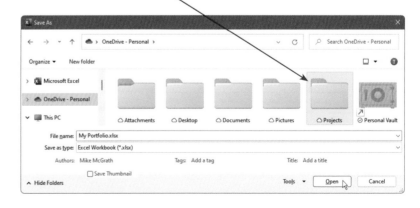

4 Amend the workbook name if required, then click **Save**

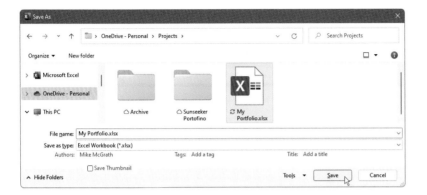

Once you have saved the workbook to your OneDrive, you should close it from within Excel if you are planning to open it from within your browser (see pages 182-183).

You can now access the workbook in OneDrive – even on devices that do not have a copy of the Excel application installed.

5 Go online to **microsoft365.com** and sign in using the email address that is associated with your Microsoft account

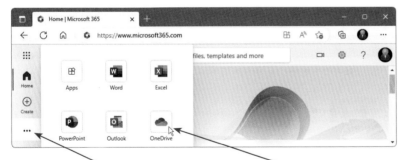

6 Click the **...** ellipsis button, then select the OneDrive icon

At the Microsoft 365 Online website you can work with documents from Word, Excel, PowerPoint, and OneNote, whether or not you have Office on your computer.

Using the Excel Online App

1 Having opened OneDrive, click the folder that contains the workbook you want to view

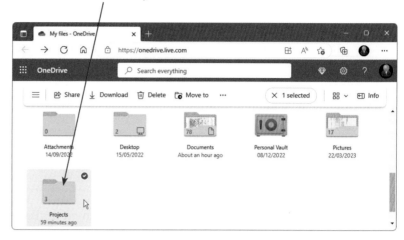

Hot tip

If you have a Microsoft 365 subscription you get a generous 1TB of free storage on OneDrive.

2 When the folder opens, right-click the workbook to display the options that are available

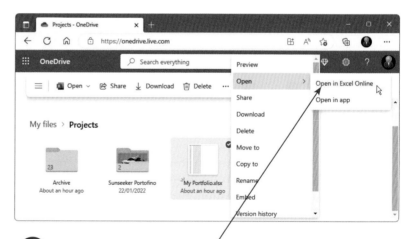

Hot tip

You can right-click a file or folder in OneDrive and select **Share** to send a link by email to allow other users to access the workbook via their browser or Excel app.

3 Select the **Open in Excel Online** option or click the **Open** menu item and choose **Open in browser**

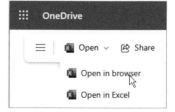

4 The workbook opens in your web browser, ready to edit

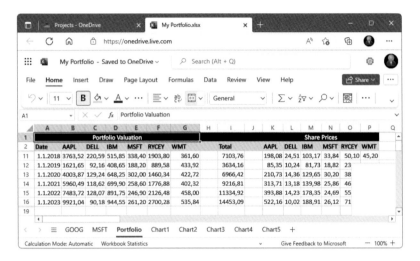

Hot tip

Any edits you make to a workbook – either with Excel Online or with the Excel app – are instantly applied to the workbook.

5 Back in the **Projects** folder, right-click the workbook and choose **Open in app** , or click the **Open** menu item and choose **Open in Excel** to switch to the desktop Excel app

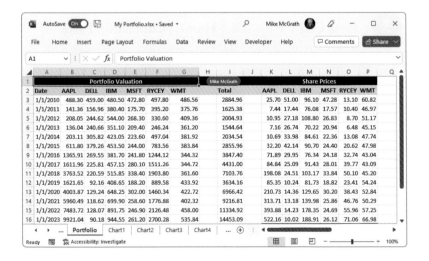

Don't forget

You need a supported version of Microsoft Excel on your computer to open the workbook in the Excel app. If necessary, you can install a trial copy.

Excel in Word

To add data from an Excel worksheet to a Word document:

1 In Excel, select worksheet data and press **Ctrl + C** (or select **Home**, [**Clipboard**], **Copy**) to copy data

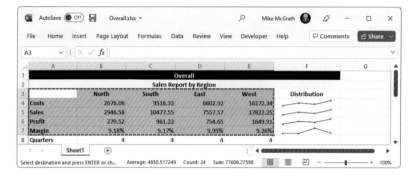

2 In Word, select the point in a document at which you want to insert Excel worksheet data

3 Press **Ctrl + V** (or select **Home**, [**Clipboard**], **Paste**) to insert the worksheet data

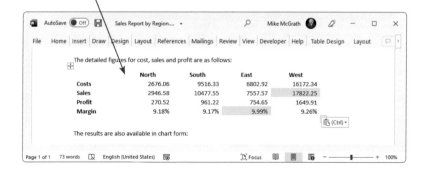

Hot tip

To share data with others who don't have access to Excel or the Microsoft 365 Online apps, you can present the information in a Microsoft Office Word document or in a PowerPoint presentation.

Don't forget

You can paste the data as a table, retaining the original formatting, or you can add formatting using styles in the Word document.

4 To copy an Excel chart to your Word document, select the chart on the worksheet, then press **Ctrl** + **C** to copy it

Apply any text styles or chart formatting required, before you copy the chart to the clipboard.

5 In Word, select where you want to insert the chart

6 Now, press **Ctrl** + **V** to insert the chart

You can also select **Paste**, **Paste Options** in the Word **Home** tab's [**Clipboard**] group and choose to paste the chart as a **Picture**, or **Keep Source Formatting & Embed Workbook**, or **Use Destination Theme & Link Data**, or **Keep Source Formatting & Link Data**.

Publish as PDF (or XPS)

To send data to others who do not have Excel or Word, you can publish the workbook in Adobe Acrobat PDF format (or XPS format) – the recipient only need have any suitable viewing app.

1 Open the workbook in Excel, optionally select an area of data, then click the **File** tab and choose **Save As**

2 Edit the file name and set the file type to PDF (or to XPS), then click **More options...**

You can publish the entire workbook, the active worksheet, or selected ranges of cells as PDF or XPS documents.

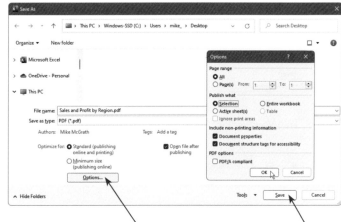

3 Click the **Options...** button to set the scope (e.g. **Selection** or **Entire workbook**) and click **OK**, then click **Save** to publish the Excel data in your chosen format

If you save your workbooks as PDF (or XPS) files, you can be sure that the files you share retain exactly the data and format you intended.

Index

Symbols

A

B

C

189

X

Y

Z